Learning zANTI2 for Android Pentesting

Dive into the world of advanced network penetration tests to survey and attack wireless networks using your Android device and zANTI2

Miroslav Vitula

BIRMINGHAM - MUMBAI

Learning zANTI2 for Android Pentesting

First published: August 2015

Production reference: 1260815

Published by Packt Publishing Ltd.
Livery Place
35 Livery Street
Birmingham B3 2PB, UK.

ISBN 978-1-78439-504-9

www.packtpub.com

Credits

Author
Miroslav Vitula

Reviewers
Manish Chauhan
Jack Miller
Fatih Ozavci
Vincent "BetaBugish" Swarte

Commissioning Editor
Kartikey Pandey

Acquisition Editor
Aaron Lazar

Content Development Editor
Adrian Raposo

Technical Editors
Tejaswita Karvir
Edwin Moses

Copy Editors
Janbal Dharmaraj
Dipti Mankame
Jonathan Todd

Project Coordinator
Kinjal Bari

Proofreader
Safis Editing

Indexer
Priya Sane

Graphics
Sheetal Aute

Production Coordinator
Komal Ramchandani

Cover Work
Komal Ramchandani

About the Author

Miroslav Vitula is a freelance graphic and motion designer and occasional Android developer with a great passion for network security. For years, he has been interested in penetration methods, exploits, and attacks done using Android devices. He explains the principles of methods used by professional network security managers and shows their usage on local networks. Some of his knowledge can be found on his blog and YouTube channel, *Android Hackz*, where he constantly adds new tips, tricks, and reviews about all Android-related things.

Huge thanks to Aaron Lazar and Adrian Raposo for helping and guiding me through the entire process of writing a book, and also to my book reviewers, Jack Miller and Fatih Ozavci, who have provided a professional feedback while writing the book. Thanks to the Zimperium team as well for making such a useful and great application.

About the Reviewers

Manish Chauhan was born in Sunder Nagar, a small town in Himachal Pradesh. Since his childhood days, he has had a great interest in technology, and he always wanted to be a developer. This was his childhood dream and he worked hard on it during his schooldays. He studied the C and Java languages neglecting his studies and so scored fewer marks in all subjects. He lost interest in the outer world and was in love with the digital world. After his matriculation, he did his polytechnic diploma in computer science, but left it and planned to complete HSC because it was hindering his childhood dream. At this point of time, he has finished +2 and is now pursuing further education from Emblem Education. He owns two websites and one android app, which are exclusively designed and developed by him. These sites and app are named *The Hacker*. You can find his blogs at www.ThaHacker.in.

Jack Miller has been working on a YouTube channel called JackkTutorials since September 2011 covering programming, hacking and security, and game servers. Since 2011, he has accumulated over 4 million video views worldwide. His hacking and security tutorials have been very popular on his YouTube channel, which has led to further exploration in the subject and more videos covering topics such as Kali Linux, Burp Suite, Wireshark, SSLStrip, and zANTI.

Jack has also worked on other books in the past with Packt Publishing, such as *Kali Linux Network Scanning Cookbook*, *Kali Linux CTF Blueprints*, and many more, and hopes to continue doing so in the future and expand his knowledge.

Fatih Ozavci is a security researcher and a principal security consultant with Sense of Security. He is the author of *Viproy VoIP Penetration Testing Kit* and *MBFuzzer Mobile Application MITM Fuzzertool*. Fatih has discovered several previously unknown security vulnerabilities and design flaws in Unified Communications, IMS, IPTVMDM, and SAP-integrated mobile application environments for his customers. He has completed several unique penetration testing services and commercial trainings during his career of more than 15 years. He also handled project lead role for several penetration testing and security research projects in Europe and the APAC area. His current research is based on attacking mobile VoIP clients, VoIP service-level vulnerabilities, mobility security testing, hardware hacking, and MDM analysis. Fatih has presented his VoIP and mobile research at HITB Singapore 2015 , BlackHat USA 2014 , DefCon 23, 22, and 21, Cluecon 2013, and Ruxcon 2013. Also, he has provided VoIP and mobility security trainings at the Defcon 23, AusCert 2014, Kiwicon 2015, and Troopers 2015 events. Refer to his homepage: http://viproy.com/fozavci.

Vincent "BetaBugish" Swarte is a Full Stack developer. He is self-employed (`http://www.vinsert.nl`) and a freelancer for Ridemi (`http://www.ridemi.nl`) and ArosaMedia.

I am grateful to Gaia, my beautiful girlfriend, for being in my life and being patient with me working over time. I am also grateful to Alex, my dad, for bringing me into the 'magical' world of computers at an early age and Heidi, my mother, for taking great care of me in the early stages of my life.

www.PacktPub.com

Support files, eBooks, discount offers, and more

For support files and downloads related to your book, please visit www.PacktPub.com.

Did you know that Packt offers eBook versions of every book published, with PDF and ePub files available? You can upgrade to the eBook version at www.PacktPub.com and as a print book customer, you are entitled to a discount on the eBook copy. Get in touch with us at service@packtpub.com for more details.

At www.PacktPub.com, you can also read a collection of free technical articles, sign up for a range of free newsletters and receive exclusive discounts and offers on Packt books and eBooks.

https://www2.packtpub.com/books/subscription/packtlib

Do you need instant solutions to your IT questions? PacktLib is Packt's online digital book library. Here, you can search, access, and read Packt's entire library of books.

Why subscribe?

- Fully searchable across every book published by Packt
- Copy and paste, print, and bookmark content
- On demand and accessible via a web browser

Free access for Packt account holders

If you have an account with Packt at www.PacktPub.com, you can use this to access PacktLib today and view 9 entirely free books. Simply use your login credentials for immediate access.

Table of Contents

Preface

This is a complete guidebook to zANTI2 application for Android. Learn how to exploit vulnerabilities, hijack passwords, perform advanced scanning on a network, and many more operations using your Android device.

What this book covers

Chapter 1, *Introducing Android Pentesting with zANTI2*, as the chapter name explains, introduces the basics of Android network penetration testing, shows you some examples of software, and essentially introduces the application interface and functions.

Chapter 2, *Scanning for Your Victim*, focuses on network mapping and Nmap scans, which are very important in network penetration testing.

Chapter 3, *Connecting to Open Ports*, explains more about open ports and its usability in penetration tests, connecting to computers remotely using various clients, and more.

Chapter 4, *Vulnerabilities*, explains how to detect and essentially exploit a remote vulnerability on a server or a computer.

Chapter 5, *Attacking – MITM Style*, guides you through the various techniques for attacking a remote machine using zANTI2. This includes password hijacking, image replacement, and many more operations.

What you need for this book

You will need a rooted Android device with a complete BusyBox installation included and the zANTI2 application.

Who this book is for

The book is intended for not only those who want to know more about network penetration tests and does not have any experience, but also for the people who are experienced in network systems and are curious to discover more about this topic. Since zANTI2 features an extremely intuitive and easy to control interface, it doesn't require any special skills.

Conventions

In this book, you will find a number of text styles that distinguish between different kinds of information. Here are some examples of these styles and an explanation of their meaning.

Code words in text, database table names, folder names, filenames, file extensions, pathnames, dummy URLs, user input, and Twitter handles are shown as follows: "A DELETE request removes all the current representations of the target resource."

A block of code is set as follows:

```
<script type="text/javascript">

window.onload=function() {
    rotate();
}

function rotate() {
    \$("img").rotate(180);
    \$(":image").rotate(180);
}
</script>
```

When we wish to draw your attention to a particular part of a code block, the relevant lines or items are set in bold:

New terms and **important words** are shown in bold. Words that you see on the screen, for example, in menus or dialog boxes, appear in the text like this: "If the option **Allow remote connections to this computer** is ticked, we're good to go."

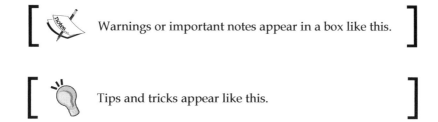

Warnings or important notes appear in a box like this.

Tips and tricks appear like this.

Reader feedback

Feedback from our readers is always welcome. Let us know what you think about this book—what you liked or disliked. Reader feedback is important for us as it helps us develop titles that you will really get the most out of.

To send us general feedback, simply e-mail `feedback@packtpub.com`, and mention the book's title in the subject of your message.

If there is a topic that you have expertise in and you are interested in either writing or contributing to a book, see our author guide at `www.packtpub.com/authors`.

Customer support

Now that you are the proud owner of a Packt book, we have a number of things to help you to get the most from your purchase.

Errata

Although we have taken every care to ensure the accuracy of our content, mistakes do happen. If you find a mistake in one of our books—maybe a mistake in the text or the code—we would be grateful if you could report this to us. By doing so, you can save other readers from frustration and help us improve subsequent versions of this book. If you find any errata, please report them by visiting `http://www.packtpub.com/submit-errata`, selecting your book, clicking on the **Errata Submission Form** link, and entering the details of your errata. Once your errata are verified, your submission will be accepted and the errata will be uploaded to our website or added to any list of existing errata under the Errata section of that title.

To view the previously submitted errata, go to `https://www.packtpub.com/books/content/support` and enter the name of the book in the search field. The required information will appear under the **Errata** section.

Piracy

Piracy of copyrighted material on the Internet is an ongoing problem across all media. At Packt, we take the protection of our copyright and licenses very seriously. If you come across any illegal copies of our works in any form on the Internet, please provide us with the location address or website name immediately so that we can pursue a remedy.

Please contact us at copyright@packtpub.com with a link to the suspected pirated material.

We appreciate your help in protecting our authors and our ability to bring you valuable content.

Questions

If you have a problem with any aspect of this book, you can contact us at questions@packtpub.com, and we will do our best to address the problem.

1
Introducing Android Pentesting with zANTI2

A few years ago, nobody really knew how far hacking could go, and hijacking a Facebook session was a piece of cake. Nobody cared much about HTTPS, personal data was easily exposed, and security was overall poor. People at the mall could be seen browsing the Web, exposing their personal information, ready to get their data stolen. Internet banking was almost *bleeding edge*; you could hijack a password and nobody would know. The boss at his office is looking for a brand new car he's going to buy from the money he got from his employees, thinking nobody will notice, though the whole squad is hijacking through an unprotected protocol seeing what the boss is up to. That might be a fun thing to do, but in fact, this can get very serious in some ways.

In this chapter, we'll:

- Talk about what goes into penetration testing
- Learn how zANTI2 fits in the picture
- Learn what is required to perform penetration tests
- Go through the zANTI interface and run through its basic functions

Penetration testing

A penetration test (or pentest, if you wish to call it that), is some sort of intrusion, or attack, that is intended to uncover weakness, security issues or vulnerability of a local network, for instance.

In this book, we will focus on Android penetration tests. We won't be focusing on these tests for exploiting Android vulnerabilities and proving insufficient security in the system, but on those network tests that are done using an Android device. As you might know, there is a whole bunch of network penetration tools for Linux-powered operating systems, including Kali Linux (formerly BackTrack) and there's a good amount of Android tools as well.

Here's a screenshot from DroidSheep, a very popular app in the past for its simple user interface and high functionality, though it was capable of only one feature—session hijacks. The app didn't have a fully working SSL strip, but we'll get to that. Actually, there was no big need for SSL back then. Most of the protocols were HTTP and open for hijacks.

This finally gets us to penetration tests and mainly, their role in networking, OS, security and basically anywhere else. If it weren't for penetration tests, there would be massive attacks due to unpatched vulnerabilities, exploited security holes, and stolen data, from hackers who just were smart enough to find and exploit some random vulnerability in the system.

That said, we need penetration tests, period.

Getting to know the dark side of Android

Android uses a Linux core since it's a Linux-based OS. Since Linux is very flexible, we can do nice things to it, not in terms of changing live wallpapers, rather about permissions: root permissions, to be precise. Heard about them? Probably yes, as you're going to need these for pentests.

The fact that your Android device is rooted may actually be caused by an exploited vulnerability in the OS. If you've ever tried to root your device running Android 2.3 Gingerbread, you've probably heard about GingerBreak software. This application ran an exploit that tried to obtain root. When succeeded, the exploit then remounts the system as R/W and runs an installer script to do the job. Superuser binary is installed, along with the well-known superuser app, and it reboots the system. Boom, easy. Most *one-click root* apps work like this by exploiting a vulnerability that leads and provides better access to the system.

Besides root access, you'll need the Swiss knife of Unix, BusyBox.

BusyBox is a utility that combines all Unix utilities and commands that are not commonly used in Android (so they aren't there) and lets you install all of these in one package.

By typing `busybox` inside of the terminal you notice how many commands BusyBox features with. BusyBox installation is a necessity for us to run network attacks and perform penetration test on a network.

Since our little penetration application uses quite a few utilities available in BusyBox, be sure to have it fully installed on your Android. BusyBox can easily be installed from one of the BusyBox installers available in the Google Play store, just search for BusyBox and you should be good to go.

To avoid any problems, I recommend that you use the BusyBox application by Stephen (Stericson) developer; it works seamlessly. The following screenshot displays the BusyBox application's download screen:

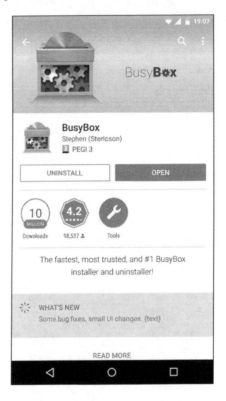

One of the most advanced penetration testing tools for Android, the very well-known dSploit, was created a few years ago. It was capable of some crazy stuff. Here's the list of some of game changing features that really moved the Android penetration testing game forward:

- Inspector (inspects the target, specifies OS, and more)
- The vulnerability finder
- The login cracker

- Man-in-the-middle attacks, including redirect, image/video replacement, JavaScript Injector or custom filter that changes text values on the Web

These are just a few features that made dSploit an awesome tool. A few years later, the main developer of dSploit joined Zimperium, a company offering enterprise class protection for mobile/tablet devices against advanced mobile attacks. They made some really good tools, which include:

- zIPS
- zConsole
- zANTI

zIPS aims to protect your device as much as possible, alerts you when there's an attacker around trying to hijack your passwords, or just performs a TCP scan of your device. zIPS also automatically keeps you safe and protects against the attack. zConsole takes all the reports from zIPS or zANTI and shows them in a nice interface on your desktop. If you're interested in taking the network security to a higher level, you can protect yourself and order these tools on `http://www.zimperium.com/`.

And then, there's zANTI—the reason why you're here reading these lines.

zANTI2

Alright, now on to zANTI2. If you've ever tried to use dSploit, you probably know that zANTI has quite similar features (some unchanged, some updated, and some new). So, how should we start?

I'd say fire up zANTI! Hang on a second! You might not have it downloaded, right? Well, if you don't have it yet, the link is `https://www.zimperium.com/zanti-mobile-penetration-testing` (input your e-mail in the field, the application link will be sent to your address).

Before you hit the **Install** button, be sure to have the unknown sources option enabled.

This can be done in the security section of settings: open settings, go to security and tap unknown sources button—enabling this option will let you install applications that are not published in the Google Play store, which is, generally speaking, pretty dangerous—considering you might install a harmful application that will try to steal your personal information.

However, this won't happen in our case, zANTI2 is a safe app and doesn't come with any malware whatsoever. The reason it's not available on Google Play is that it does not meet the requirements. For your security, don't forget to disable this option back, or simply install apps from Google Play store only.

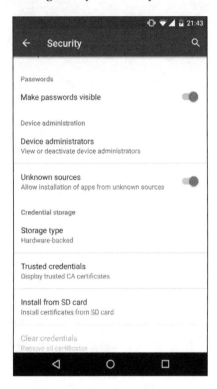

Once **Unknown sources** option is checked, you will be able to install applications that do not come from the official Google Play store, but from other sources as well. Since zANTI2 is not available on Google Play, assure this option is checked.

Done installing? Good! Open the app and be sure to grant the superuser permissions so that it can execute commands as root. Otherwise, the application will not work. Also, ensure that everything you need is properly installed—talking about BusyBox. Sit back and get ready to zANTI.

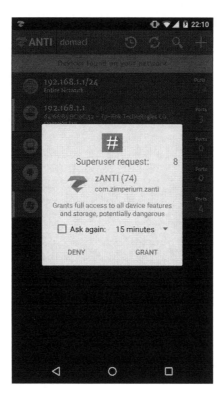

zANTI2 needs superuser privileges to work. Be sure to grant the full access, otherwise zANTI2 will not be functional.

Run through the initial setup, accept the terms of use, and grant superuser permission.

Let's take a first look at zANTI2's interface and explain the basic functions.

We'll start from the top. The action bar shows you SSID — the name of a network you're connected to. Pretty useful stuff! Moving on, now we have the History button. Tapping this gets you to another window showing the networks you connected to along with the targets that were found during the scan. It will also show you the number of open ports and IP and MAC addresses. This might come in useful when gathering information about networks you connected to in the past.

Right next to the History button is a map network function. We will talk about this more in the following chapter as it's very important and needs more pages to fully explain the whole idea of it.

The next button is Search; it lets you find a device on a network by inputting its IP, MAC address, or a name.

The last button adds a host to the network, which can be useful for adding hosts from the **Wide Area Network (WAN)** and performing further actions on them; for example, you can check for remote vulnerabilities such as ShellShock or Poodle.

The rest you see in the middle is a result of a completed scan—displaying targets on a network. Every target has an IP address followed by a MAC address and occasionally a name.

The little round icon on the left represents the OS running on a target—Windows, Linux, or Android. It also shows you the type of a target, whether it's a computer, network router, or a device. The icon you see on the top indicates the *entire network*. When selected, any further action will affect every single device on the network.

Then, there's the distributor of the target, Apple, Huawei, Samsung, Intel, HTC—even this is something that gets captured by a quick network mapping.

The number you see on the very right is the number of open ports on the target. Open ports are very important for us, as we will use these numbers to find out further information and connect to them, and if they show any signs of vulnerabilities, run exploits on them.

Moving on. You can access more *little* features by swiping your finger to the right. These are not the main, primary, or even new functions to the network penetration tools, though they might come in very useful and mostly, they're here, making zANTI2 an even more complete and compact application.

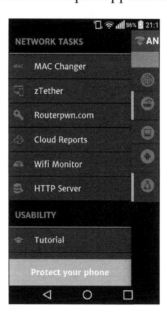

Mac Changer

As you can see, we have a few more things to explore. Starting with network tasks, the MAC Changer does what it says; it simply changes your MAC address. MAC addresses are identifiers of each node of a specific network. You've probably signed up to networks, in airports for example, which will let you use the Internet connection for only 30 minutes or so. After you reach the limit your MAC address gets banned from the network, thus you can't use it anymore.

Changing your MAC address might in some cases give you 30 more minutes for a quick browse through the net.

A certain company once used special trash bins to track people's movement around the city based on their MAC addresses. This is possible because your MAC address gets broadcasted even if you're not connected to any network.

Ever heard of the app, Pry-Fi?

Pry-Fi aims to make your device as safe as possible, changing your MAC address every once in a while. The app also comes with something known as a *War mode*, which makes your device appear like it's a dozen people. This, according to the author's words, will flood the tracking data with useless information and possibly reduce the tracking that is being done on an everyday basis. Pry-Fi randomizes your MAC address, following a pattern *that still makes the trackers think you are a real person, but they will not encounter your MAC address again.*

That said, if you're not feeling safe enough, definitely check this app out, it comes free and is available on Google Play Store.

zTether

Moving on to zTether. Ever shared your mobile data connection to your friends? Well, this little feature lets you play with them a bit.

zTether offers full tether control by executing the MITM type of attacks, including redirect, a replace images feature, download interception, and every other feature that zANTI has to offer. We'll be talking about the MITM attacks in *Chapter 5, Attacking – MITM Style.*

RouterPWN

The next feature, coming with a pretty fancy name, is RouterPWN. RouterPWN is a web application that uses and exploits various vulnerabilities in devices such as routers, access points, or switches.

It allows you to run local or remote web exploits, allows offline exploitation, and runs smoothly even on a mobile web browser, making it a really interactive tool for lots of penetration stuff.

For example, RouterPWN is capable of converting SSID to wireless key (WEP) for Thomson SpeedTouch ST858 v6 models. So if your neighbor seems to use this kind of router, you might want to let him know his security status by doing some MITM magic on his network. RouterPWN is a great tool for security purposes, finding vulnerabilities in your network and making your network much more safe to use.

As seen in the preceding screenshot, RouterPWN opens in a nice mobile web, which makes it really practical and even easy to use. That said, clicking on this in the zANTI app opens the URL for you, letting you further interact with this awesome tool on the Web.

Cloud reports

The next function is the so-called **cloud reports**. We will not be using cloud reports, since this requires zConsole. Let's move on.

The Wi-Fi monitor

The Wi-Fi monitor shows a list of all available Wi-Fi networks in range. There's also a nice implementation of scanner, which shows the intensity of each network.

You can see a little bookmark-like marker that changes color depending on network security—green for secured, red for open ones; showing us that it's not a good thing to leave our Wi-Fi routers accessible to anyone—and it really isn't; we'll get to that, don't worry, this is what the book is about.

The HTTP server

Moving onto the next one, the HTTP server quickly creates an on-device HTTP server, letting you share folders/files through HTTP connections. This is useful for sharing files and the likes, but we won't be interested in this one in our penetration testing chapters.

Looks like we're done with the Network Tasks section, leaving the **Usability** section untouched. This section contains a not-so-descriptive tutorial that quickly introduces users to the interface. This is followed by the **Contact Us** button, which allows you to share your thoughts, feedback and problems if you have any.

Should we have a look at settings, or not? It's just settings. Let's move on!

Come back to the home screen. The text saying **devices found on your network** clearly suggests the list you're looking at is the list of devices that are currently connected to the Internet.

If you're not seeing anything, it might be because either nobody is connected (though you should always see your device, that's the one saying **This Device**) or because zANTI2 hasn't scanned for devices yet.

To perform a quick scan, go ahead and tap that little button next to search.

A tiny popup will appear; let's leave the **Intrusive Scan** option unselected for now and hit **OK** to start scanning. The length of time may vary, depending on the network and number of devices connected.

If your scan has finished already and you start scanning a fresh, old values will be replaced with the new ones. Therefore, if you just fired up zANTI2 after a little while, you might want to manually rescan to work with results that are up to date.

Yay! Network scan completed. If you're that type of guy, you can even tweet about your freshly-completed scan but that's completely up to you.

If you take a closer look, you'll probably see your router with an IP address, let's say 192.168.1.1. This is the default gateway and it's also the IP of the router you're most likely connected to.

Let's go ahead and click on one of your targets, the router, for example. A new window will pop up giving you further information about the target. The IP, MAC, Name of the target, and ports are included in the report.

Take a look at the **Comments** section. You see, the guys from Zimperium have thought about your great and open mind, leaving you the whole section free to express yourself. You can input words such as `Hacked this bloke a week ago,` `this guy needs a rest. Will be back in two months!`, and maybe some other types of useful stuff. Well, on a serious note, this section can be used to document and make notes of your progress.

Let's skip the middle section for now, but don't worry, we'll get back to it later.

Have a look at Nmap scan:

Nmap scan

Nmap (**Network Mapper**) is an open source utility for network discovery and scanning, available not only for Linux but also Windows, when it comes to it. It supports a wide variety of scan types, including basic scan, ping scan, UDP scan, IP protocol scan, and many more. Since we'll be talking more about scans in the following chapters, let's just say Nmap is really a great utility with huge usability especially in network pentesting.

> *"We have all seen many movies like Hackers which pass off ridiculous 3D animated eye-candy scenes as hacking. So Fyodor was shocked to find that Trinity does it properly in The Matrix Reloaded. Needing to hack the city power grid, she whips out Nmap version 2.54BETA25, uses it to find a vulnerable SSH server, and then proceeds to exploit it using the SSH1 CRC32 exploit from 2001. Shame on the city for being vulnerable (timing notes)."*

`- http://nmap.org/movies/`

Yup, the Nmap scan was even featured in the Matrix Reloaded.

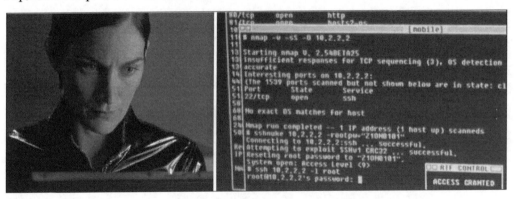

That said, let's finally move on to the middle section, which will lead us to operative and attack actions. Don't worry, we'll get to know Nmap much better in the following chapter; it's an amazing tool!

Operative actions

Operative actions are those kinds of actions where the device tries to interact or discover the target and investigate it a bit closer, whereas attack actions simply perform attacks on that target.

To explain operative actions more (scan, remote ports connection), you'll read about these two in the following chapters (*Chapter 2, Scanning for Your Victim*, and *Chapter 3, Connecting to Open Ports*). Just to briefly show you around, scan action performs a second scan, this time on the target only.

Scans, as mentioned earlier, are done using Nmap and are logged into the Nmap scan log afterwards.

Apart from having the opportunity to choose from a fine amount of scan types, including Ping scan, UDP scan, and others, you also can execute a script. You can run AUTH, BROADCAST, BRUTE, DNS, SSH, SLL, and many more types on the target, resulting in the scan-log output, where you'll be retrieving information from the target.

We shouldn't forget about a tiny feature called smart scanning, which automatically searches for exploitable vulnerabilities.

Moving to the port connection, this is one very interesting feature. zANTI2 lets you choose one of the available ports and establishes a connection to it.

We will, again, learn about this particular feature and its usability in *Chapter 3, Connecting to Open Ports*; it needs to be a bit further explained and investigated.

Let's have a look at attack actions, starting with *password complexity audit*.

Password complexity audit

The password complexity audit feature checks and eventually tries to crack access passwords for available services (SSH, for example) using available dictionaries in the app.

> The password complexity audit function uses THC Hydra. Hydra brute-force cracks remote authentication services, against more than 30 protocols, including HTTP, HTTPS, TELNET, FTP, and many more.

To crack an access password, you'll ideally need some dictionaries to crack from. The developers made it easy, leaving five preloaded dictionaries directly in the app. You can also perform a brute-force attack without using a dictionary, but this might not always be the best option. You'll see why in *Chapter 3, Connecting to Open Ports*.

Starting with a small dictionary, this one's for the shortest possible passwords. This logically takes the least amount of time; thanks to having the lowest combination of words. On the other hand, a huge dictionary contains a way greater amount of words. This will increase the probability of finding and cracking the access password, but the whole process will take way more time.

While dictionary attacks work by searching for possible words listed in the dictionary provided by the user, incremental is a brute-force attack. This kind of attack seems to be the simplest one. Simply put, it tries password combinations over and over again, until finally it gets the right one.

Logically, attempting to crack a password without using any dictionaries is the most time-demanding process because the possible combinations are generated using your phone's processor, instead of trying predefined words from a dictionary.

In case you wondered, this is how the cracked password message looks. Not the safest password now, is it?

Right below the password cracker is the well-known MITM, which is one of the spiciest features of the whole zANTI2 app. Hijacking accounts, passwords, replacing images, injecting custom JavaScript, and much more—this all is done using the Man-In-The-Middle attack. Amazing! Isn't it?

More about MITM, how it works and functions to come in *Chapter 5, Attacking – MITM Style*, (the last chapter, ending it in style.)

The last two options in attack actions are the vulnerability checks. zANTI2 currently offers checking of ShellShock and SSL Poodle.

Zetasploit

Leaving the public clueless about further development of zANTI, the Zimperium team has successfully made cloud exploits available from within the app and created something known as Zetasploit.

Using Metasploit, one of the most used penetration utilities, Zetasploit aims to run and exploit vulnerabilities based on scan results. Unfortunately, Zetasploit is available to enterprise users only and supposedly will be available for public users as well at some time. Hopefully, it is now when you're reading these lines!

You've probably seen the video showing the power of Zetasploit. (If not, look it up, it's crazy — `https://youtu.be/di5FHSh3Z7c`).

From what we know, there are over eight separate exploits (probably many more) available from the server, then there's a **client** tab followed by **file intercept**.

The guy seems to run a Windows exploit that exploits a parsing flaw in the path canonicalization code of `NetAPI32.dll` through the server service. Then, he selects an available VNC payload to connect the desktop and finally launches the exploit.

He then takes control of the entire system using the graphical interface, which was successfully provided by the VNC.

VNC is not the only option for connecting to the victim; the video also shows us how to interact with the generic shell and execute the `shutdown -r` command, which reboots the computer. Easy, peasy!

Although all of these sound very interesting, we'll probably not get our hands on them till they're officially announced in the next release. However, as you will read in *Chapter 3, Connecting to Open Ports*, regarding connecting to open ports, it is possible to intrude into a computer using port number 3389, which is responsible for remote desktop connection.

That being said, you can't run Metasploit on your Android powered device. Or can you?

Oh, of course you can! The newly-updated cSploit, which is being continuously updated by one of the former developers of dSploit has (apart from original dSploit features) slightly improved tweaks and added new features such as:

- The vulnerability finder
- The exploit finder
- Metasploit Framework integration

At least that's what `http://www.csploit.org/` says, and it looks like the app is doing really well. Since the main developer is only one person and is often busy, we can't expect frequent updates, but it's great to see that we can use Metasploit exploits using a free Android tool.

Summary

In this chapter, we learned what penetration testing is and how Android comes into the picture to perform testing over networks. We also were introduced to zANTI, and learned about its various features in brief and how effective it is in performing network penetration testing.

In the next chapter, we'll move on to learn about scanning and the different types of scan used for this purpose.

2
Scanning for Your Victim

As you might've guessed already, a scan is something essential, especially in our case of performing MITM-type of attacks and whatnot. Without completing a successful scan, we would not be able to perform a successful attack. In this chapter, we're going to:

- Learn what scanning and network discovery is
- Find out the different types of scans and categories zANTI provides
- Understand what each scan one does
- Identify which method is best suited for a particular scenario

Network discovery

Let's proceed to the stage of looking around: detecting victims and scanning. Imagine this situation as the one over a shooting range: you grab your weapon (zANTI2, in our case), aim and shoot. You have to aim for your target, obviously—otherwise, you would not hit it. The same thing applies to our case—we need to trace and find the target before we shoot. And that's what the scan does.

Now, when you're familiar with the interface of the lovely app, it should not be a problem to perform a successful scan on a target. If you're still confused about how to trigger a proper scan, let's go trough the process once more.

To avoid any confusion, there are two scan types. Both are used for scanning, but one for a general network discovery (called network mapping) and the other one for a slightly more detailed scan performed on a single target. Let's talk about the first one first, the network discovery.

Network discovery is essential, no doubts about that. Without this function, you would not be able to target the devices, computers, routers, or whatever you are trying to perform a penetration test on. You can't hit what you cannot see, right? The network discovery gives you a choice to choose one particular target or to select an entire network. It also presents you with useful information, such as open ports and the general type of device—printers, routers, phones, computers, basically anything that's connected to the local network.

The mapping network can easily be triggered by clicking the arrows icon next to the search icon on top of the app's interface.

All scanning processes are performed through the Nmap. What you'll see in this chapter is mostly zANTI2 performing various commands to trigger the Nmap power and capabilities of discovering the OS version, vulnerabilities, and every piece of information you might be interested in. Nmap is extremely useful, and in our case, an indispensable tool.

You might've noticed the **Intrusive Scan** option as one of the checkboxes inside of this little window. The intrusive scan does what it says; it scans for vulnerabilities on a host by performing test cases directly on it. Go ahead, try the Intrusive scan on your network, and see what you see going on there.

Also, notice the **Clear logs** button, which is actually more helpful than you think, removing all the old logs from the console and clearing it before writing new stuff into it. You'll understand its importance when we get the Nmap logs.

Network mapping can take a lot of time. If you're mapping a network with a bunch of devices connected to it, you might want to bring a charger to avoid losing a high amount of battery during the process. This is something you should know before scanning huge networks, it does really take a lot of time.

The network scan is complete; let's have a look at the results!

Luckily, the developers have made this particular section very well, making it easy and practical to retrieve the basic information from the network map scan.

In this case, the map discovery has found three devices hogging on the local network, one of which is my current device that I've been mapping the network with (marked as **This Device**). There's also a router device, which has three open ports on it. We can also quickly find out that the router is from TP-LINK Technologies, which can in some cases help for exploitation of numerous vulnerabilities using the Router-PWN website.

Now, when you're familiar with the network discovery, we can finally move on to the real Nmap scans, which we will be talking about in this chapter the most.

Open or closed?

I've mentioned open ports. I guess I'll explain this a bit more because this is something you should probably know before getting into the game.

Although Nmap is now one of the best scanning software out here, it started as a port scanner. It's a simple but efficient port scanner. The simple command nmap on target scans 1000 TCP ports on it. You've probably heard of *open* or *closed* ports, but in fact Nmap divides ports into six states:

- Open
- Closed
- Filtered
- Unfiltered
- Open | filtered
- Closed | filtered

First, let's explain open and closed ports. If a host is accepting **Transmission Control Protocol (TCP)** connections, **User Datagram Protocol (UDP)** datagrams, or **Stream Control Transmission Protocol (SCTP)** associations, we call this port *opened*.

Finding open ports is often the main goal of port scanning, considering that each open port is vulnerable to attacks. Hackers are attacking these, while system administrators are trying to protect them from unwanted connections using known security tools such as Firewall. In short, Firewall establishes a trusted connection between secured devices on an internal network and another, unsecured network, typically the Internet. Based on the applied rule set, Firewall controls the incoming and outgoing network traffic.

If a connection from a software is trying to be broadcasted to the Internet, Firewall simply blocks it. For instance, if you're facing a connection issue with e-mail or an IM client, then it may be possible that the port required by this application is getting blocked by Firewall.

Open ports also show services available for use on the network. There are many well-known ports that you might've heard about already, the port 80, for instance—is a HyperText Transfer Protocol, typically referred to as a HTTP port, or port with number 21—a **File Transfer Protocol (FTP)** port, which is used for file transfer between computers/devices on the local network. FTP is one of the oldest protocols, and you can also create a FTP server on your Android device using a FTP client, which can be downloaded on Google Play Store.

You might've also heard about port forwarding, which basically allows remote computers to connect to a specific computer within a private **local area network (LAN)**.

It is typically used to forward data securely from another application running on the same computer as the **Secure Shell Client**. Talking about SSH, it is possible to create a simple SSH server on your Android-powered device as well, using one of the apps available in the store

Now, let's get to closed ports. As you might've guessed already, a closed port is simply a port that isn't listening to any connection. It rejects all packets directed to it. This gives you an idea of how port scanning is important, especially for malicious hackers. You cannot remotely attack a closed port because it just refuses everything you're trying to send to this port. It's like talking to somebody who will just not listen to you, like somebody you want to hang out with, but the person says "no" every time you ask, so there's basically no opportunity.

A closed port is not interesting for a penetration tester, hacker, or cracker, whoever you are trying to be or already are. However, closed ports are accessible. Despite the person answering "no" to every question, every time you ask, it is still possible to visit and ask him.

However, they can possibly be helpful in showing that a host is up on an IP address. And because these ports are still reachable, it may be worth scanning them in case they open up in the future.

Getting to the *filtered* state, this state shows up when Nmap cannot determine whether the port is open because packet filtering prevents its probes from reaching it. This often happens because of firewall or router rules. Sometimes, these ports respond with ICMP error messages such as **destination unreachable**, but filters that simply drop probes without responding are far more common. This forces Nmap to try to scan this port over and over again in case the probe was just dropped due to network problems rather than it's just being unavailable. These ports make scanning really slow.

Unfiltered ports are generally those ports that Nmap cannot determine whether they are open or closed.

Open | filtered is the similar case. This state shows up when Nmap that performs a UDP scan is unable to determine if a port is open or filtered. This occurs when ports give no response (UDP waits for response for closed ports, but not for open ones). This lack of response could signify multiple cases and when Nmap can't say if it's the first or another one, it places the port in this state. Closed | filtered is the same story. If it's unsure about whether the port is closed or filtered, it goes in this state.

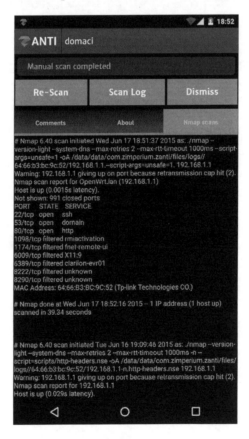

You can see the completed scan results on the previous page in the Nmap scan log, which clearly shows the presence of multiple TCP ports. Three of them are opened, SSH, domain, and HTTP, six of them are filtered, which, as you already know, might be caused either by firewall or router rules that are causing the probes to be unreachable.

Scan types

In some cases, you are looking to determine whether the host is up, and in some cases, you want to really dig deep and find out as much information as possible from the target. Sometimes, you want to detect if the OS target is running, so you can determine whether there are any possible exploits on it. Nmap offers a fine amount of scan types, which let you investigate and find the exact information just the way you want. Let's have a look at the ones available through zANTI2:

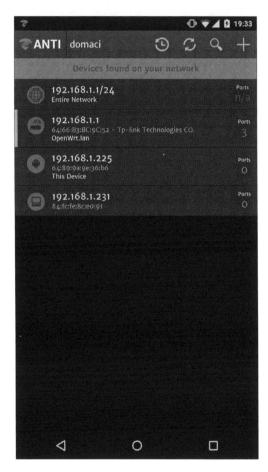

In zANTI2, the advanced scanning can be triggered for individual targets only. After you're done with network mapping, choose one of the targets and select **Scan** to perform *advanced scanning on target*, as the app says.

You'll find yourself in a new activity window with these three options. The first option, **Scan type**, lets you choose the type of scan triggered on the target. There are many scan types including regular, intense, or ping that you will get to know more about in a jiffy. The **Execute script** option appeals on the scripting engine of Nmap, which is one of the most powerful tools Nmap has to offer. Nmap is capable of executing a script (that you as a common user can write as well and publish into the Nmap script index) followed by printing the results of this script. There are many categories and script types, some of them detect and exploit vulnerabilities, some are attempting to discover more information about the host, and so on. The Nmap Scripting Engine has a very broad usability, no matter if you're a hacker, system administrator, penetration tester, or just being curious about things around networking—**Nmap Scripting Engine** (NSE) is a very powerful tool and we will dig into it a lot deeper in just a few pages.

The third option, the so-called **Smart scanning**, attempts to find a vulnerability in the outdated system version, for instance by directly executing intrusive scripts on the target.

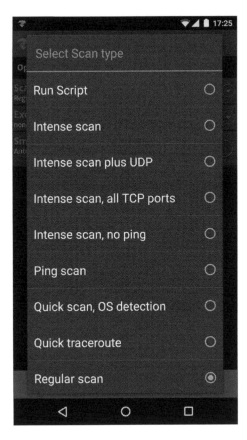

Let's have a closer look at scan types.

Each scan type is slightly different from each other, whether it's the area of scanning, or the accuracy of the scan itself. Firstly, we should probably explain what all these mean and in what situations would be the best time to use them.

Run script

Run script, as the title suggests, executes one of the available scripts. This option triggers the Nmap Scripting Engine and fires one of the scripts available from the huge index of scripts available in the Nmap archive. We'll get to this in a jiff because there's more to talk about.

Intense scan

Intense scan is a very detailed, comprehensive scan. Logically, this means the intense scan may take up much more time scanning than the others will probably take, though it may come in useful when you want accurate results. This scan does the following scans and detections to reach the most accurate result as possible:

- OS detection
- Version detection
- Script scanning
- Traceroute

Let's cover these first. OS detection does a detailed detection of operating system running on a host. Nmap does this scan by stack fingerprinting, which works by sending series of TCP/UDP packets and then monitoring the response from the target. This scan is one of the best-known scans of Nmap. More about OS detection is given on the following pages.

The version detection is, described by Nmap, a high speed, parallel the operation via nonblocking sockets and a probe definition grammar designed for efficient yet powerful implementation. Version detection determines the application name and version number where available; it supports both TCP and UDP protocol and multiple platforms, including Linux, MAC OS X, Windows, Solaris, and others.

If available, Nmap connects using SSL (if OpenSSL is present), which allows it to discover various services such as HTTPS, POP3 as well as providing version details. If the SunRPC service is discovered, a brute-force RPC grinder is launched to find the program name along with the version number. Nmap has a very comprehensive database, recognizing more than one thousand service signatures and covering over 180 service protocols such as ACAP, AFP, XML-RPC, or Zebra. You've probably asked yourself if it is really important to determine the exact version type and number on the target? Yes, it is—obviously this helps in determining which exploit the target is vulnerable to. Another good reason is that multiple services can share the same port number—for instance, a TCP port 258 is used by both the Checkpoint Firewall-1 GUI management interface and the Yak Windows chat client. This makes a guess based on the `nmap-services` inaccurate. Also, you can often find services listening to unregistered ports (a registered port is a network port defined within the Internet Protocol, in the range of 1-65535 for use with a certain protocol or application)—these unregistered ports are a mystery without version detection. The next thing is that filtered UDP ports can often look the same as open ports. But if they respond to the specific probes sent by Nmap version detection, you can be 100 percent sure that these ports are open.

The result from a completed version scan would look like this:

```
PORT     STATE   SERVICE   VERSION
22/tcp   open    ssh       OpenSSH 4.3 (protocol 2.0)
```

Let's move on to the script scanning, which is also involved in the Intense scan. Script scanning is normally done in combination with a Port scan because scripts may be run or not run, depending on the port states. Script scanning involves the **Nmap Scripting Engine** (**NSE**) and directly executes the most common scripts while scanning. To specify and run a custom script in zANTI2, simply run the Script Execution and select your desired script. The scripts executed during the Intense scan are included in the default set of scripts (in Nmap defined as -sC or -script=default) and these are mostly the ones that finish quickly (this excludes force authentication crackers, web spiders, and scripts performing brute-force attacks). Default scans are meant to produce valuable, actionable, and easy-to-understand information about the target. These scripts are often the most reliable ones and none of them are intrusive, meaning they belong to the *safe* category and they're not trying to exploit or find any vulnerability in the system.

A typical script that's executed during the Intense scan is nbstat, which attempts to retrieve the target's NetBIOS names and their MAC addresses. The script displays the name of the computer and the logged-in user along with all names the system thinks it owns. The result would look like this:

```
Host script results:
|  nbstat: NetBIOS name: WINDOWS2003, NetBIOS user: <unknown>, NetBIOS
MAC: 00:0c:29:c6:da:f5 (VMware)
|  Names:
|    WINDOWS2003<00>        Flags: <unique><active>
|    WINDOWS2003<20>        Flags: <unique><active>
|    SKULLSECURITY<00>      Flags: <group><active>
|    SKULLSECURITY<1e>      Flags: <group><active>
|    SKULLSECURITY<1d>      Flags: <unique><active>
|_   \x01\x02__MSBROWSE__\x02<01>  Flags: <group><active>
```

The result is, as always, saved into the Nmap scans log that you can access anytime during the scan.

The last scan type involved in the Intense scanning is traceroute.

Generally speaking, traceroute is a utility that records the route through the Internet between your computer and a specified destination computer. Traceroute also calculates the amount of time each hop took.

This utility is a handy tool and is widely used, mostly for finding problems in the network. Traceroute works by sending a packet (using the Internet Control Message Protocol or ICMP), including a time limit known as the **time to live** (**TTL**) that limits the lifespan of data in the network. This enables traceroute to determine the exact amount of time required for the hop to the first router. Values are then printed along with the hops.

Have a look at the traceroute result in the Nmap log inside of zANTI2:

The distance is 1 hop with **round-trip delay time** (**RTT**) of 13.30 ms. RTT marks the length of time it takes for a signal to be sent plus the length of time it takes for an acknowledgment of the same signal to be received.

This all is being found in one scan. Besides these detections, the Intense scan also scans TCP and UDP ports.

 UDP stands for user datagram protocol and TCP means transmission control protocol.

UDP uses a simple transmission model and has no handshaking dialogues, thus is often marked as unreliable with no guarantee of delivery, ordering, and such. Then there's TCP, commonly referred to as TCP/IP, thanks to its complementation to **Internet Protocol** (**IP**). Many internet applications and services rely on this protocol, such as the **World Wide Web** (**WWW**), e-mail, or file transfer.

If a service does not require a reliable but fast data stream, UDP is used — thanks to its connectionless transmission model.

We distinguish four types of Intense scan:

- Intense scan
- Intense scan plus UDP
- Intense scan, all TCP ports
- Intense scan, no ping

The *Intense scan plus UDP* does exactly the same thing as the Intense scan does (OS detection, version detection, script scanning, and traceroute), in addition to scanning TCP and UDP ports. While most popular services on the Internet run over the TCP protocol, UDP services are widely deployed. The most common are DNS, SNMP, and DHCP. UDP scanning is generally slower—open and filtered ports rarely send any response, leaving Nmap to time out and then conduct retransmissions in case the probe or response were lost.

UDP scan works by sending a UDP packet to every target port. Occasionally, a service will respond with a UDP packet, proving that this port is open. If no response is received, this port is marked as open | filtered. In this case, the version detection is used to differentiate the ports that are actually opened.

Intense Scan, all TCP ports does again, the same thing as the Intense scan and also scans all TCP ports—leaves no TCP port unchecked. Normally, Nmap scans a list of 1000 most common protocols, but in this case, Nmap scans every port from 1 to 65535.

Followed by *Intense scan, no ping*, this scan does exactly the same as the Intense scan without checking to see whether targets are up first. This type of scan can be useful in situations when a target seems to ignore the usual host discovery probes or if it's blocking ping request and you already know that the target is up.

Before proceeding to next scan types, let's explain the OS detection, that is an essential part of the Intense scan.

OS detection

OS detection is one of the best-known features in Nmap. This scan is used by TCP/IP stack fingerprinting—your phone sends a series of TCP and UDP packets to the victim and carefully examines the response given from it. Nmap then compares the results with more than 2000 known OS fingerprints. Then, this finds out any matches and prints them into your log.

If you take a look at the log in the previous screenshot, you can clearly see the results are pretty accurate—I am indeed running Windows 7 Professional.

Now, you may be asking yourself whether these OS scans are really that important and useful?

OS detection is mainly used for finding out vulnerabilities, more precisely, reducing false positives of exploits on the targets. For instance, if a certain OS version contains an unpatched vulnerability, you can run an OS scan to find out which targets are vulnerable.

On the other side, as a system admin, OS detection provides a really easy way to search for vulnerable targets in your network and patch these before hackers exploit them. OS scans can also prevent hacker attacks caused by unprotected networks. If an employee in a big company installs a wireless access point on the network, this might just start a new threat for the company. Nmap even has a special category for WAPs, so as a system administrator, you can safely detect unauthorized devices like these before bad guys do.

Several things are being determined using this detection. Let's have a look at them.

These are parts of the OS detection that are collecting information based on the fingerprints. There are eight of them:

- Device type
- Running
- OS CPE
- OS details
- Uptime guess
- Network distance
- TCP sequence prediction
- IP ID sequence generation

All of these items are safely stored in the scan log, where you can view the results.

It is now more than obvious that OS detection plays a big role in the game, helping you detect outdated software that might be vulnerable to attacks. Let's take a closer look at the individual parts listed above and explain what they mean for us.

Take a look at a result of the OS detection scan done on my laptop.

```
Device type: general purpose|phone
Running: Microsoft Windows 7|Phone|Vista|2008
OS CPE: cpe:/o:microsoft:windows_7::-:professional cpe:/
o:microsoft:windows cpe:/o:microsoft:windows_vista::- cpe:/
o:microsoft:windows_vista::sp1 cpe:/
o:microsoft:windows_server_2008::sp1
OS details: Microsoft Windows 7 Professional, Microsoft Windows
Phone 7.5, Microsoft Windows Vista SP0 or SP1, Windows Server 2008
SP1, or Windows 7, Microsoft Windows Vista SP2, Windows 7 SP1, or
Windows Server 2008
Network Distance: 1 hop
```

For the best and most accurate scan results, Nmap has to find one open and one closed port. If not found, Nmap can still provide and show some results but they might not be reliable and accurate.

Let's have a look at these one by one.

Device type

All fingerprints that are examined by Nmap carry a general type of device (target)—this might be router, firewall, printer, or general purpose device—here, we can see the target listed as general purpose/phone. If Nmap is unsure about multiple results, it will show both of them, separating these with the pipe symbol (router | firewall).

Running

This line shows the OS family and if available; it also shows the OS generation (Linux 2.4.x, for instance). When Nmap cannot narrow down the generations, multiple OSes can be listed, divided by a pipe symbol. If Nmap finds too many OS families, it will omit this line. When there are no perfect matches for the OS family, Nmap adds an accuracy percentage (where 100 percent is a perfect match) after each possible candidate. If Nmap finds no close matches to fingerprints, the line is omitted.

OS CPE

OS CPE shows **common platform enumeration (CPE)** of the OS. CPE is a standardized way to name software apps, OSes, and hardware platforms. CPE typically contains seven fields:

```
cpe:/<part>:<vendor>:<product>:<version>:<update>:<edition>:
<language>
```

Some fields, however, can be left blank or even left off. If you take a look at the preceding screenshot, you can see there are five fields listed, one of which is left blank.

You may be wondering what does the o stands for in the `cpe:/o:` field in the beginning.

To clarify *O* stands for operating systems, *A* for applications, and *H* for hardware platforms. If you take a look at the picture, it lists four possible OSes. It's clear that the target is running Windows 7 Professional operating system, which turns out to be correct. Moving on!

OS Details

This line gives the details about each (matched) fingerprint. If there are multiple matches, all of these are listed and separated by comma (have a look at the image). If there are not any perfect fingerprint matches, the field is renamed to `Aggressive OS guesses` and fingerprints with a percentage of accuracy of matches are shown.

Network distance

Network distance lists how many routers are between you and your target—the distance for localhost is 0, 1 for a device on the same network segment. Each additional router on the path adds one *hop* to the count. Again, the line is omitted if Nmap cannot compute it (due to no reply to the relevant probe).

Uptime guess

Not visible on the preceding screenshot, but still a part of OS detection, Nmap tries to determine the approximate uptime of the remote system. Nmap receives several SYN/ACK TCP packets in a row and checks the headers for a timestamp option. Many operating systems use a simple counter starting with zero at boot time and counting during the uptime. By checking the responses, Nmap can determine these values and print these in the scan log.

The uptime guess is marked as a `guess` because there are several things that can make it very inaccurate. For instance, some operating systems do not start the counter at zero but initialize it with a random value instead.

TCP sequence prediction

It is possible to make a full connection to a system with a poor TCP initial sequence number and perform a blind TCP spoofing attack on them. This kind of attack was the most popular one in the '90s when people used `rlogin`, which is a remote shell client (like SSH) that allows users to log in on another host via network, communicating using TCP port number 513. In December 1994, Kevin Mitnick had supposedly used this attack to break into Tsutomu Shimomura's (computer security expert, currently CEO of Neofocal Systems) computers. Luckily, almost nobody uses `rlogin` anymore. However, blind TCP spoofing may still be effective for HTTP requests.

```
TCP Sequence Prediction: Difficulty=259 (Good luck!)
```

Now, you might be surprised with the log. What does the *good luck* comment mean? Well, there is an estimated difficulty of how hard the system makes blind IP spoofing (where 0 is the easiest).

These comments are based on this index, starting from *trivial joke* to *easy*, *medium*, *formidable*, *worthy challenge*, and finally ending with *good luck*.

IP ID sequence generation

This field describes the ID generation algorithm recognized by Nmap, showing a possible vulnerability (to TCP Idle scan, for instance) in the system. However, many systems use a different IP ID for each host they communicate with. In this case, they may appear vulnerable while in fact being secure against the attacks.

Have a look at the scan results of the Intense scan. If you look carefully, the Nmap log shows many more then expected. Notice the port scan, showing four open ports, two of which have been diagnosed with version numbers.

Also, notice the warning line saying the OS scan results may not be reliable because Nmap was not capable of finding at least one open and one closed port.

If a message like this shows up, keep in mind that the OS scan loses its accuracy.

The uptime shows up to be somewhere around two days, which in this case, seems to be quite correct.

Let's move on to the other scan types. Whereas the Intense scan is the most comprehensive and accurate one, there are many more that, in some cases, you'd prefer using over the Intense scan.

Let's have a look at Ping scan.

Ping scan

Ping scan is a quick type of scan that only finds out whether the target is up—it does not scan for ports.

```
# Nmap 6.40 scan initiated Sat May 30 21:09:41 2015 as: ./
nmap --version-light --system-dns --max-retries 2 --
max-rtt-timeout 1000ms -sn --script-args=unsafe=1 -
oA /data/data/com.zimperium.zanti/files/logs//64:66:b3:bc:
9c:52/192.168.1.1-sn. --script-args=unsafe=1. 192.168.1.1
Nmap scan report for OpenWrt.lan (192.168.1.1)
Host is up (0.014s latency).
MAC Address: 64:66:B3:BC:9C:52 (Tp-link Technologies
CO.)
# Nmap done at Sat May 30 21:09:42 2015 -- 1 IP address
(1 host up) scanned in 0.14 seconds
```

This scan is potentially useful in situations when you're unsure whether the target is up or not to perform more time-consuming actions on it and not waste the time waiting for the results.

In this case, the host seems to be up with 0.014 s latency. In case you don't know, latency is the delay from input into a system, to the desired outcome. We generally recognize three types of latency: Internet, WAN, and Audio latency.

Quick scan and OS detection

Quick scan is slightly faster than the Intense scan by limiting the number of TCP ports scanned to only the top 100 most common TCP ports and by using a more aggressive timing template. This scan, also known as **quick scan plus** also performs OS detection along with the version detection (that was explained a few pages ago). The best example of usage would be mainly for the OS detection itself, as it's the fastest way to retrieve OS and version info in the shortest amount of time, considering the other scans (Intense and Comprehensive scan) take more time.

Quick traceroute

Quick traceroute traces the paths to target; it does not perform a scan on them. Traceroute is included in the Intense scan and is mostly used for network analysis.

```
TRACEROUTE
HOP RTT    ADDRESS
1  13.30 ms OpenWrt.lan (192.168.1.1)
```

As mentioned, the RTT marks the length of time it takes for a signal to be sent plus the length of time it takes for an acknowledgment of the same signal to be received. In Microsoft Windows, the traceroute is included by way of the `tracert` command, which basically does the same on websites, tracking the response time redirections. Traceroute is often used by hackers, who use this tool to map the network nodes and get general information about the whole net architecture, making it easy to find and investigate a weak link on the network area. This is one of the reasons some webs block traceroute through utilities such as Firewall to prevent this easy network mapping on the whole net.

Slow comprehensive scan

You can guess by its name that this scan will take a bit more time than all the other ones. This is the most accurate and comprehensive scan of all the scans available, with every TCP and UDP being scanned and all minor scans and detections being enabled, including OS detection, version detection, script scanning, and traceroute.

This is a highly intrusive scan, which uses three different protocols in order to detect the hosts: TCP, UDP, and **SCTP (Stream Control Transmission Protocol)**.

This scan, unlike others, will not give up if the initial ping request fails and will try as much as possible to identify the host by using every possible method. This scan smartly camouflages itself as port 53, which is the port number for **Domain Name System (DNS)**.

IP/ICMP scan

Since ICMP doesn't have a port abstraction, this cannot really be considered port scanning. This scan, however, might be useful to determine what hosts are in a network by pinging them all. ICMP scan is usually quite fast as well.

Here's an output found in the log:

```
PROTOCOL STATE  SERVICE
1       open   icmp
6       open   tcp
7       closed cbt
32      closed merit-inp
58      closed ipv6-icmp
68      closed anydistribfs
70      closed visa
83      closed vines
84      closed ttp
98      closed encap
112     closed vrrp
150     closed unknown
200     closed unknown
210     closed unknown
215     closed unknown
217     closed unknown
222     closed unknown
224     closed unknown
235     closed unknown
240     closed unknown
241     closed unknown
249     closed unknown
```

Talking about ICMP, I should probably explain this protocol a bit more. ICMP is one of the main and most important protocols used by network devices. It is typically used to relay query messages or to send error messages indicating a service is not available or when a datagram cannot reach its destination, for example. Basically, the ICMP is an error reporting utility. Each ICMP message is comprised of three fields that define its purpose. These are TYPE, CODE, and CHECKSUM. The TYPE field consists of eighteen different parts, each with its own description for the error that the message is referring to. For instance, TYPE 1 means that the destination is unreachable; TYPE 5 is a redirect message; and TYPE 12 means parameter problem. Recently, the Zimperium Mobile Security Labs team has discovered new ICMP redirect attacks in the wild from all over the world in 31 different countries. This attack, called *DoubleDirect*, is a type of MITM attack and will be explained in detail in the last chapter of the book.

Script execution

We're getting to probably one of the most interesting parts—the script execution. The Nmap Scripting Engine is one of its most powerful and best-known features that Nmap itself has to offer. Nmap offers a ton of user-written codes available to use worldwide. NSE aims to provide highly sophisticated network discovery, vulnerability, and backdoor detection, and obviously also its exploitation.

Many of the scripts that Nmap has to offer have obviously also been ported and can be used in the zANTI2 app on your Android device, which provides you with a great way to perform penetration tests without need of a computer—all your tools now are available in your pocket.

Script execution in zANTI2 is a really easy thing to do. Select a host, tap on scan (just the way you did to perform an OS scan), and instead of pulling a ping, ICMP, traceroute scan, OS detection, simply tap the **Execute scan** button.

Every executable script in Nmap belongs to its own category. There are nine main categories available through zANTI2 with loads of scripts contained in each of these.

The categories are AUTH, BROADCAST, BRUTE, CITRIX, DATABASE, DISCOVERY, DNS, GEOLOCATION, and INFO. The Nmap Scripting Engine offers a fine amount of scripts, where some are meant for general discovery, gathering more information about a particular host, and some used to remotely detect vulnerability and possibly even exploit it. Let's have a closer look at each of these categories.

As mentioned earlier, each category covers a particular task performed on the target. NSE supports four types of scripts, distinguished by the kind of targets they are executed on and the scanning phase in which the scripts are run. The types are:

- Prerule scripts
- Host scripts
- Service scripts
- Postrule scripts

Prerule scripts run before any of Nmap's scan phases. These scripts can be useful for tasks such as performing network broadcast requests because they don't depend on specific scan targets.

Host scripts are run after Nmap has performed host discovery, port scanning, version detection and OS detection on the host. An example would be `whois`, which looks up additional information for a target IP.

Service scripts run against specific services listening on a target host. For instance, Nmap includes over 15 HTTP service scripts to run against web servers. If a host has web servers running on multiple ports, those scripts can be executed and run multiple times for each port.

Postrule scripts run after Nmap has scanned the entire target. A potential use of these scripts is printing a reverse index of the output, showing which hosts run a particular service (rather than only listing the services on each host).

Let's have a look at categories. Nmap Scripting Engine divides each script into its appropriate category, making it easy to find, distinguish, and execute the script you're looking for. Currently, there are fourteen defined categories, but zANTI2 shows fifteen of them, some of which are not even listed in the Nmap index. Let's take a look at them and see what zANTI2 has to offer.

Auth

These scripts deal with authentication credentials on the target. A typical example is the `x11-access` script, which checks whether you're allowed to connect to a server. If this server is listening on a specific TCP port, it's possible to check whether you're able to get connected to the remote display by sending an initial connection request. Basically, these scripts do not attempt to brute-force the credentials, instead they try to bypass them. Scripts that use the brute-force method are listed in the **Brute** category instead.

Broadcast

Scripts in this category discover hosts that are not listed on the command line by broadcasting on the local network. For instance, broadcast-dropbox-listener prints all the discovered client IP addresses, names, and version numbers of Dropbox accounts by listening for the information broadcasts sent on the local area network that is being done every 20 seconds.

Brute

As the title **Brute** suggests, these scripts use brute-force attacks to guess authentication credentials of a server. Nmap contains scripts for brute-forcing dozens of protocols, including http-brute or oracle-brute. Scripts in this category are logically intrusive, as they are attempting to directly hack into a server. A typical example is http-brute script, which performs password auditing against basic HTTP authentication.

> Brute force is an attack when a device tries to guess a password, for example, by trying all possible combinations till the right one is found. This can obviously take a lot of time, depending on the speed and complexity of the password.

If we have a look at the output of pop3-brute script, which tries to log into a POP3 account (POP3 is a Post Office Protocol and is used for grabbing e-mail messages from a remote client, working through a TCP/IP connection.), we could see something like this:

```
PORT    STATE SERVICE
110/tcp open  pop3
| pop3-brute-ported:
| Accounts:
|   user:pass => Login correct
| Statistics:
|_  Performed 8 scans in 1 seconds, average tps: 8
```

This script lists the port (typically 110 for a POP3 service), state, and service along with the final output carrying the results. Statistics for the attack are listed as well showing the number of performed scans and average number of TPS.

Citrix

Citrix scans are used mainly against Citrix XML services. Citrix Systems is a software company providing server, application, and desktop virtualization and cloud computing technologies. Scripts such as `citrix-enum-servers` attempts to extract the name of the server along with member servers from the Citrix XML service. There also is a script called `citrix-brute-xml` that attempts to brute-force and find valid credentials for the Citrix PN Web Agent XML Service. This category isn't listed in the default Nmap index, but it was created in zANTI2 because all of the scripts included in this category are used against Citrix services. Most of the scripts (`citrix-enum`) listed in this category are otherwise included in the **Discovery** category as they mostly attempt to discover further information about the host.

Database

These scripts are used against two databases: MS SQL and MySQL. Scripts such as `ms-sql-brute` performs password guessing against the Microsoft SQL server. Another script, `mysql-databases`, for example, attempts to list all databases on a MySQL server. In other words, this section lets you play and investigate on these two databases. Again, this category isn't listed in the Nmap index by default, but zANTI2 has it probably for the sake of clarity. In case you don't know what these two databases mean, MS SQL (or Microsoft SQL Server) is a database system developed by Microsoft. Its primary function is to store and retrieve data requested by other software applications. MySQL is again, a database system, currently the world's second most used one. MySQL is currently a very popular choice of database for use in a web application and is widely used among many companies, including YouTube, Twitter, Facebook, and Google.

Discovery

Discovery scripts, in general, try to discover more about the network by querying public registries, SNMP-enabled devices, directory services, and more. Scripts in this category are not intrusive and they don't try to exploit or find any vulnerability in the system. Most of these scripts are marked `default`, which means they are being executed during one of the scans I've covered several pages ago (for instance, OS detection scripts are executed during the Intense scan). Examples include the `html-title` script, that obtains the title of the root path of websites or `snmp-sysdecr`, that extracts system details via **SNMP (Simple Network Management Protocol)**.

DNS

The DNS category deals with DNS check scans, brute-force attacks, client subnet scans, and more. Examples include the `dns-blacklist` script that checks target IP addresses against multiple DNS anti-spam and open proxy blacklists and returns a list of services for which an IP has been flagged. In case you don't know, DNS stands for Domain Name System. If you want to visit Google, you can type `google.com` into your browser's address bar. However, the browser doesn't quite know where `google.com` is, for this IP addresses are used (in our case, this would be 173.194.39.78 for Google). DNS can be explained like a phone book, DNS matches names to numbers for easier interaction with items listed in it.

Geolocation

Geolocation contains a category of scripts that are, based on IP addresses, trying to determine the location of the host using available services such as Geobytes or Geoplugin. Scripts such as `ip-geolocation-geobytes` uses `http://www.geobytes.com/` to identify the physical location of an IP address, the `ip-geolocation-geoplugin` script uses `http://www.geoplugin.com/`. While this might not sound like a big deal, geolocation is generally used by companies mainly for analytics and statistics for determining the location of a viewer or visitor. In case you're curious about how geolocation works, services that use this have access to a number of databases that provide them the information for locating someone online through an IP address. A primary source for IP address data is the Regional Internet Registries. These are very large organizations responsible for managing IP addresses in specific regions of the world. There are five Regional Internet Registries in the world: ARIN for American Registry, RIPE NCC for Europe, APNIC for Asia, LACNIC for South America, and AfriNIC for Africa. The geolocation services then simply narrow down the area finally ending up with your exact location.

Protocol

The Protocol category lets you execute a script to a wide variety of protocols: **AFP (Apple Filing Protocol), APJ (Apache JServ Protocol), FTP (File Transfer Protocol)**, HTTP, IPv6, **LDAP (Lightweight Directory Access Protocol), RDP (Remote Desktop Protocol), SIP (Session Initiation Protocol), SMTP (Simple Mail Transfer Protocol)**, and **SNMP (Simple Network Management Protocol)**. Simply put, if you're looking for a script performing actions on a particular protocol, this is the category you would choose to quickly search for the script. Scripts in these under-categories might be *safe* (meaning they are not intrusive and will not crash any services during the investigation) but they may also be intrusive and actively searching for vulnerabilities, such as the `afp-path-vuln` script, which detects the Mac OS X AFP directory traversal vulnerability.

Info

Info includes a wide variety of various scripts that retrieve usable information about targets. The `Acarsd-info` script, for instance, uses the **ACARS (Aircraft Communication Addressing and Reporting System**) and decodes the data in real time. Information retrieved from this script includes the daemon version, API version, admin e-mail, and listening frequency (yes, we're talking about airplanes). Generally speaking, scripts in this category provide additional information about hosts in every possible way.

Then, there are a few more categories with more or less usable scripts. For example, `bitcoin-getaddr.nse` lists known as Bitcoin nodes or `skypev2-version.nse`, detects the Skype version 2 service. Irrespective of whether it is useful or not, these examples clearly show that anybody can code a custom Nmap script that will do its thing, whatever that might be.

However, the Nmap index of script categories lists several more categories with interesting scripts, and some of them appear to be available through zANTI2. Categories such as *intrusive*, *exploit*, or *vuln* are clearly used for penetration test purposes, as their primary task is to detect vulnerabilities in the system and possibly even exploit it, printing out all the information that the exploited vulnerability has to offer to us.

Let's have a look directly at the scripts that are available in zANTI2 that you can execute right from your Android device.

Brute-force scripts

These scripts simply perform a brute-force attack, usually to find out login credentials, against servers, databases, services, protocols, just about anything that could potentially give you any spicy information. Thus, they are all intrusive and *kicking*. Have a look at the list:

- `Backorifice-brute`: This script performs a brute-force attack on the Back Orifice service. Back Orifice is a computer program designed for remote system administration. In short, it lets a user control a computer running Windows OS from a remote location. It's old but it works.

- `Cassandra-brute`: This does the same thing, brute forcing—this time the Cassandra database. Cassandra is a very reliable database management system designed to handle large amounts of data, with the lowest possible amount of fails.

- `Metasploit-msgrpc-brute`: This performs an attack against the Metasploit `msgrpc` interface. (Metasploit, for those that don't know, is one of the most complete, best known penetration software for Windows/Linux. It's currently the world's most used penetration testing software.)

- `Metasploit-xmlrpc-brute`: Once again, this script performs a brute-force attack on a Metasploit RPC server using the XMLRPC protocol.

- `Imap-brute`: This performs brute force against IMAP servers using either LOGIN, PLAIN, CRAM-MD5, DIGEST-MD5, or DLM authentication. These are methods that servers can use to negotiate credentials (talking about username and password) using a web browser.

- `Oracle-brute`: This performs the attack against Oracle servers—does an audit of common Oracle usernames and passwords.

- `Pop3-brute`: Tries to log into a POP3 account (you can access a mailbox using the POP3 or IMAP protocol, POP3 is the most commonly used one) by simply guessing usernames and passwords.

- `Smb-brute`: This attempts to guess username/password combinations over SMB.

- `Telnet-brute`: This performs a brute-force attack against telnet servers.

- `Vnc-brute`: This one is against **VNC (Virtual Network Computing)** servers. VNC is a graphical sharing system that is used to remotely control another computer. It transmits the keyboard and mouse movement from one device to another over a network. If you've ever tried to connect to your computer using your Android-powered device, you probably used the VNC Viewer app to remotely view the desktop and control it via this app.

- `Domcon-brute`: This performs password auditing against the Lotus Domino Console.

- `Membase-brute`: This performs attack against Couchbase Membase servers.

- `Mmouse-brute`: This performs password auditing against the RPA Tech Mobile Mouse servers. Mobile Mouse, if you haven't heard, is a tool that enables remote control of the mouse (and keyboard) from an iOS device. Pretty cool, and what's better, you can brute-force it!

- `Netbus-brute`: This performs the attack against the Netbus backdoor service.

- `Nping-brute`: This performs a brute-force attack against the Nping Echo s Service.

- `Omp2-brute`: This is an attack against the OpenVAS manager using OMPv2.

- `Redis-brute`: This performs a brute-force attack against a Redis key-value store.

- `Rexec-brute`: This is an attack against the Unix rexec service.

- `Rlogin-brute`: This does an attack against the Unix rlogin service. If you remember, `rlogin` was used by Kevin Mitnick to break into a large computer network.

- `Xmpp-brute`: This performs an attack against XMPP instant messaging servers.

Broadcast scripts

Scripts in this category broadcast in the local network to find out information, attempting to discover services by sending queries, for instance. These scripts are mostly marked `safe` by the Nmap index, as they are not attempting to exploit any remote vulnerability on the remote host.

- `Broadcast-dns-service-discovery`: This tries to discover hosts' services using the DNS Service Discovery protocol.

- `Broadcast-dropbox-listener`: This script listens for the LAN sync information broadcasts that are being done by `http://dropbox.com/` every 20 seconds. The script then prints all the discovered client IP addresses, port and version numbers, displays names, and more.

- `Broadcast-netbios-master-browser`: This discovers master browsers and the domains managed by them.

- `Broadcast-novell-locate`: This attempts to use the Service Location Protocol to discover Novell NetWare Core Protocol servers.

- `Broadcast-pc-anywhere`: This sends a broadcast probe to discover pcAnywhere hosts on a local network. pcAnywhere is a suite of computer programs that allows a user to connect to a personal computer running the pcAnywhere host if both are connected to a local network.

- `Broadcast-ping`: This sends broadcast pings using raw Ethernet packets and outputs the responding hosts' IP and MAC addresses.

- `Broadcast-wake-on-lan`: This script wakes up a remote system from sleep by sending a **WoL (Wake-on-LAN)** packet. WoL functions are very popular nowadays. If allowed, you can even turn on a switched off computer by sending this packet through the network.

- `Broadcast-listener`: This sniffs through the network for incoming broadcast communication and attempts to decode all the received packets, supporting many protocols, including Spotify, DropBox, **CDP (Cisco Discovery Protocol)**, DHCP (**Dynamic Host Configuration Protocol**), **ARP (Address Resolution Protocol)**, and more.

- `Broadcast-ms-sql-discover`: This script discovers Microsoft SQL servers in the same broadcast domain.

- `Broadcast-pppoe-discover`: This discovers PPPoE servers using the PPPoE Discovery protocol. The PPPoE stands for Point-to-Point protocol over Ethernet and it's a network protocol that is used to connect multiple computer users on an Ethernet local area network to a remote site through common equipment. For instance, the PPPoE can be used by multiple employees in an office to share a common DSL, cable modem, or wireless connection to the Internet.

- `Broadcast-rip-discover`: This script does a host and routing information discovery from devices running RIPv2 on the LAN by sending a RIPv2 request and again, collects the responses from the hosts. RIPv2 is one of the most common routing protocols in use today.

- `Broadcast-ripng-discover`: Again, this script discovers host and routing info from devices running **RIPng (Routing Information Protocol, Next Generation)** on the LAN. The difference between RIPv2 and RIPng is that RIPng is a version of the RIP modified for use with **IPv6 (Internet Protocol Version 6)**. RIPng runs over UDP.

- `Broadcast-tellstick-discover`: This discovers Telldus Technologies TellStickNet devices on the local area network. If you haven't heard, TellStick is a handy USB-stick radio frequency transmitter that plugs into your computer, turning it into a wireless home automation center by creating a link between your computer and all the electronic devices, such as lights.

Info scripts

If you ever want to retrieve some more information from a host, you might want to execute the info scripts. Here are some that you could potentially find useful:

- `Bitcoinrpc-info`: With Bitcoin getting more and more common among users and companies, this script will obtain information from a Bitcoin server by simply calling the `getinfo` command on its JSON-RPC interface. The script outputs balance, blocks, connections, difficulty, hashes per sec, version, and more.

- `Cassandra-info`: This retrieves info and server status from a Cassandra database.

- `Ipv6-node-info`: This shows hostnames, IPv4 and IPv6 addresses through IPv6 node information queries.

- `Mysql-info`: This prints out information such as the protocol and version numbers, status, capabilities, and more.

- `Cups-info`: This lists all the printers managed by the CUPS printing service, shows model, DNS-SD name, state (stopped, processing, idle) and how many print jobs are left to be done.

- `Broadcast-upnp-info`: This attempts to extract system information from the UPnP service. UPnP is used for automatic discovery of Plug n Play devices on the network.

- `Metasploit-info`: This gathers information from the Metasploit RPC service. This outputs host name, OS name, version, manufacturer, build type, and many more.

- `Quake3-info`: This extracts information from a Quake3 game server. Alright, you probably won't need this one.

Intrusive scripts

Here are a few examples of intrusive scripts that are checking and possibly exploiting vulnerabilities in the system. This category of scripts will probably be the most interesting to you, as it's important and necessary to continuously check for *holes* in the network to avoid any potential harm caused by hackers.

- `Firewall-bypass`: This script detects vulnerabilities by spoofing a packet from the target server. The vulnerability is located in the netfilter and other firewalls that use helpers to dynamically open ports for protocols such as **FTP (File Transfer Protocol)** and **SIP (Session Initiation Protocol)**.

- `Jdwp-inject`: This one attempts to exploit Java's remote debugging port. When this port is left open, it's possible to perform an injection and achieve remote code execution.

- `Samba-vuln-cve-2012-1182`: This checks whether the target machine is vulnerable to the Samba heap overflow vulnerability CVE 2012 1182. This vulnerability allows remote code execution as the *root* from a completely anonymous connection.

- `Domino-enum-users`: This attempts to discover valid IBM Lotus Domino users and download their ID files by exploiting the CVE-2006-5835 vulnerability. (The version before 6.5.5 FP2 and 7.x before 7.0.2 does not require authentication to perform user lookups, which allows remote attackers to obtain the user ID file.)

- `Distcc-cve2004-2687`: This detects and exploits a remote code execution vulnerability in the distributed compiler daemon Distcc. Distcc is a program designed to distribute compiling tasks across a network to participating hosts. The vulnerability was disclosed in 2002, but it still can be present in modern implementations due to poor configuration and maintenance of the service.

The following scripts are used against **Server Message Block (SMB)** found in the SMB category in zANTI2. The SMB protocol provides a method for applications in a computer to read and write to files from server programs in a computer network. It is mainly used for providing shared access to files, printers, or serial ports and other communications between nodes on a network.

- `Smb-check-vulns`: This script checks for the following vulnerabilities in the SMB:
    - MS08-067: This is a Windows RPC vulnerability.
    - Conficker: This is an infection by the Conficker worm, which infected millions of government, business, and home computers in over 200 countries.
    - Unnamed regsvc DoS: This is a denial-of-service vulnerability, which has been accidentally discovered in Windows 2000.
    - SMBv2 exploit: This allows remote attackers to execute arbitrary code or cause a system crash using the DoS attack.
    - MS06-025: This is a Windows Ras RPC service vulnerability.
    - MS08-029: This is a Windows Dns Server RPC service vulnerability.

- `Smb-flood`: This exhausts a remote SMB server's connection limit by opening as many connections as possible. Most SMB implementations have a global limit of total 11 connections for user and 10 for anonymous connections. The script exploits this limit by making up and holding the connections.

- `Smb-vuln-ms10-054`: This checks whether the target machine is vulnerable to the MS10-054 SMB remote memory corruption vulnerability. The SMB server in Microsoft Windows XP SP2, SP3, Windows Server 2003 SP2, Windows Vista SP1 and SP2, Windows Server 2008 Gold SP2, R2 and Windows 7 does not properly validate fields in an SMB request, which allows attackers to execute arbitrary code via a crafted SMB packet.

- `Smb-vuln-ms10-061`: This checks whether the target is vulnerable to MS10-054 *Spooler impersonation* vulnerability. This script checks for the vulnerability in a safe way without any possibility of crashing the remote system as this is not a memory corruption vulnerability. The Print Spooler service in Microsoft Windows XP SP2, SP3, Windows Server 2003 SP2, Windows Vista SP1 and SP2, Windows Server 2008 Gold (SP2 and R2) and Windows 7, when printer sharing is enabled, does not properly validate spooler access permissions, which allows for the creation of files in a system directory and execution of code by sending a print request over RPC. (RPC, or Remote Procedure Call is used for creating client or server programs. It allows client and server software to communicate).

The following scripts are used against **SMTP (Simple Mail Transfer Protocol)**.

SMTP is a protocol that moves e-mails across networks to send the communication to the right computer and e-mail inbox.

- `Smpt-vuln-cve2010-4344`: This script checks and possibly exploits a heap overflow based on the CVE-2010-4344 vulnerability, which allows an attacker to execute arbitrary code via an SMTP session that includes two mail commands in conjunction with a large message containing crafter headers, leading to improper rejection logging. In Exim Version 4.72 and prior (Exim is a message transfer agent), the script also exploits CVE-2010-4345 vulnerability, which allows local users to gain special privileges.

- `Smpt-vuln-cve2011-1720`: This checks for a memory corruption in the Postfix SMTP server when it uses Cyrus SASL library authentication mechanisms. This vulnerability, marked CVE-2011-1720, allows denial-of-service attacks and remote code execution.

- `Smpt-vuln-cve2011-1764`: This looks for a format string vulnerability in the Exim SMTP server with DKIM (DomainKeys Identified Mail, a tool detecting spoofed e-mails using public keys and signatures). When exploited, attackers can execute arbitrary code or cause a daemon crash using the DoS attack via format string specifier.

Summary

In this chapter, we learned what scanning is and how important it is in penetration testing. We also learned about the various tools that zANTI offers for scanning, showed the most important scripts available for execution through the powerful Nmap Scripting Engine, which does its job perfectly and puts the power of desktop computers into your hand.

In the next chapter, we'll discover some useful techniques done on the open ports and how it's possible to connect to these using zANTI's port connection feature and ConnectBot, which will provide a way to connect to Secure Shell servers and open ports.

3
Connecting to Open Ports

Connecting to open ports is one of the many ways to establish some sort of a link between the target and your hacking machine. zANTI2 lets you do this in a really nice and simple way, letting you further interact with your target based on services and port numbers.

In this chapter you're going to:

- Learn more about the open ports
- See how the connection between the target and your device is established using ConnectBot and zANTI2
- Learn how to connect to a specific open port on a remote machine
- Learn how a password-protected protocol is cracked using a brute force or dictionary attack

Open ports

Open ports are extremely important, especially for further control with a remote system. An open port is a clear sign of activity and broadcast on a target system, and having multiple ports open indicates several things. Firstly and mainly, it's generally not safe to have all ports open in terms of security. Some ports can be accessible through various network connections and be insecure for potential attacks coming out of the device environment, as we will show in the next pages.

If you read the previous chapter carefully, you probably have an idea of how easy it is to exploit a vulnerability in suitable conditions using a wide variety of scripts offered by the **Nmap Scripting Engine** (**NSE**). The point is, if you leave a port open and accessible, the device accepts anything that is sent to it, even malicious communication requests coming from attackers. Therefore, you could say that your primary goal to increased security would be to have all ports left closed, so the device does not accept any network packets from the network. This, however, would be difficult, since many services are using various ports to communicate, for instance the remote desktop port, which we will be attacking.

As you probably know, this is why we use a firewall to implement network control for us and protect our computers against unauthorized network access.

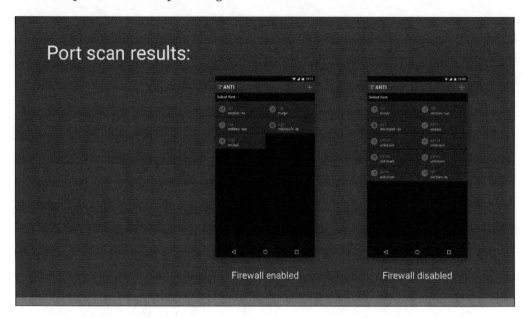

On the preceding image you can see how a firewall limits the number of open ports. The result is not surprising: it is obvious that there will be many more open ports accessible on the host with a firewall disabled. If you look closely at the picture, you should notice that the ports exposed with a firewall disabled have a slightly higher number than the other port numbers. You might be asking yourself, does this matter? Well, let's have a look at what numbers generally mean.

There are three categories for port numbers:

- Privileged ports (0-1023)
- Registered ports (1024-49151)
- Dynamic, private, or ephemeral ports (49152-65535)

The privilege ports, sometimes also called simply **common** or **system ports**, are the ports used by system processes that provide widely used types of network services. For instance, port 22—**Secure Shell (SSH**—used for secure logins, file transfers, and port forwarding) or typically port 80, the HTTP port.

Registered ports are those ports that are used for a specific service, for example AutoNOC protocol (port 1140) or OpenVPN (1194). Registered ports are assigned by **IANA (Internet Assigned Numbers Authority)**.

Then there are dynamic ports, ranging from 49152 to 65535. These ports are not registered with IANA and services using these ports are mostly used for private services and client connections.

Ports are also either official or unofficial, depending on whether the port is registered with IANA or not. If you have a look back at the picture on the previous page, you'll notice there's a port carrying a very high number (49152), meaning it's private and thus unofficial and unregistered. But why is it there and what service does it represent? Well, this port is used by `wininit.exe` on Windows machines and it is a system file that is often called a **Windows startup application**. Ports like these are blocked with a firewall so the bad guys cannot connect to them and thus cause any harm.

Talking about hacking, the process of intruding and poisoning a port is actually simple. For example, using User2Sid and the NetBIOS auditing tool, it is possible to hack a wide variety of ports including 139, 138, 137, 136, 135, and 445. After determining whether any of the ports are open, a null session to the target session is created. By using User2Sid you can easily identify a valid user and its **Security Identifier (SID)** on a Windows system. Then the admin account password is cracked using the brute force auditing tool. Conclusion? Close as many ports as possible.

I've mentioned port forwarding a few times here and this should be explained as well. Your Internet provider assigns exactly one IP address to your Internet connection. This means you have multiple devices in your house but only one address. In short, port forwarding provides a way to tell the router what computer inside your network incoming connections should be directed to. Let's take port 80, used for HTTP. If an incoming packet arrives, saying that it is carrying number 80, it means that this port must be a request for a web server. All incoming connections with matching numbers will be forwarded to the specific computer with the request thanks to port forwarding.

A typical example would be a multiplayer game, where port forwarding is commonly used. If you create a game server letting other people from the Internet connect and play with you, your computer doesn't know which players want to join you so it cannot establish a connection to them. Instead, players have to send connection requests to you. This is where port forwarding helps to sort things out.

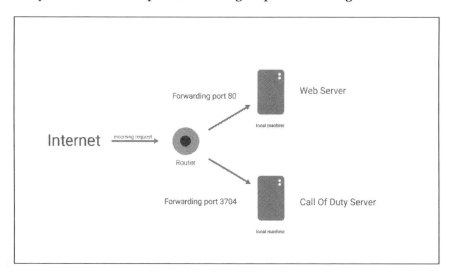

Here's a simple scheme of practical use. Two machines on a local network share the same router but run two different services: one is running the **CoD** (**Call of Duty**) server, and the other one the web server (ports 80 for HTTP and 3704 for the CoD server). Ports are forwarded for different services so the incoming requests hit the right machine. That's it.

As mentioned in the second chapter, every scan performed in zANTI2 is done through Nmap. Again, even open ports are discovered using this tool. Despite the fact that Nmap is very good at discovering open ports, be sure to always wait for the network mapping process to finish, so every single port is found. If Nmap doesn't finish its mapping process, some open ports may stay undiscovered and you will not be able to connect to these ports in the future. Think of a shooting range—aim accurately, then shoot.

Connecting to open ports

We're getting to the next stage of establishing a stable connection between our target, a remote machine on a local network, and devices. There are various ways and types of connections, with zANTI2 offering many of them.

The type of connection varies with every port. With some ports the connection is only indicating a port is active; however, some ports can be dangerous for the target itself. The type of connection depends on the port type. For instance, establishing a connection to SSH port 22 with a router lets you execute Linux commands on the target, which then allows you to list the directories or change the access password.

However, the connection can be password-protected. For instance, you're probably using a password on your desktop PC or laptop. While you're using this password protection to stop people accessing your machine, the network may be a much more dangerous place.

Let's start from the beginning. Start by network mapping the whole local area to discover every possible open port on the host you're trying to connect to. It is possible to manually select a port in case you are sure that it is open, but for the sake of having all the ports discovered, it is better to wait until the process is completed.

Since the number of open ports is the primary goal of your scan, you can leave **Intrusive scan** unchecked for faster scanning.

When the mapping is done, a number of open ports should appear. Open your target and navigate to **Operative Actions**:

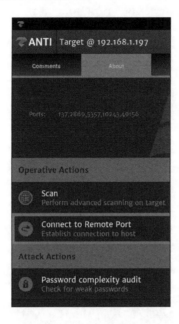

In **Operative Actions**, select the **Connect to Remote Port** option. A list of all found open ports will appear as follows:

We got these five open ports where two of them are unknown. What about the other ones? **Port 137, netbios-ns,** for instance, is used by NetBIOS name service port (also known as WINS Service). Although almost any machine with NetBIOS enabled and not configured properly is considered dangerous, the only thing we could potentially do on this port (in our case) is to connect to it. There are vulnerabilities that can be exploited through this port, so let's do it! Tap port **137** and wait a few seconds until it connects. Now, since zANTI2 doesn't have an SSH client—integrated, you'll have to download one first. zANTI2 will probably redirect you to download ConnectBot, which is a fast and stable SSH client. If you're already using some other client, JuiceSSH for example, you can stick with it.

After connecting to a port like this, you haven't got many options left. The connection clearly indicates the port is open and accepts the packets you're broadcasting. Congratulations, you've established a connection between your machine and a remote port. If you're thinking about hacking a computer using NetBIOS, it is theoretically possible but the target would have to be extremely vulnerable and exposed, having no firewall, **File, and Printer sharing** enabled. Generally, this isn't the best option to invade a remote machine:

But we're not done here yet. There are a few more ports that are way more interesting for us.

Let's take a look at port number **22**, which is the SSH port. SSH, or Secure Shell, is a network protocol for securely getting access to a remote computer. SSH is commonly and widely used by network administrators to control servers using classic Unix commands and it also provides functions such as file transfer, IP tunneling, and more. When SSH's login is used, the entire login session including transmission of the password is encrypted, which makes it really hard to collect these passwords. SSH also protects a network from attacks such as IP spoofing, DNS spoofing, and more (IP spoofing is sending network packets from a specific IP address—even the real owner has no access to it—to a target system). Although SSH is fairly safe (there is still a risk of exploiting an insecure connection, performing brute force attacks, and more), we can still connect to it. With cracked login credentials, it is possible to execute remote commands to list directories and change the access password completely.

As the image on the right shows, a **Username** with a **Password** are required to establish a connection to the SSH port. Now, we have multiple options to connect to the port. We can launch a password-complexity audit—brute force the password or perform a dictionary attack using implemented dictionaries in the application or by using a custom one. However, this is where most security provisions fail. These credentials may often be ridiculously secure, having only the basic password to secure the SSH. In some cases, the password is the same as the username. For instance, the username and password *oracle* is one of the most used combinations. This is followed by *root*, *password*, *admin*, or simple combinations like *123456* or *abc123*. If you're lucky enough, you can guess the credentials right away. If not, Hydra comes to the fore.

Cracking passwords

THC Hydra is one of the best-known login crackers, supports numerous protocols, is flexible, and very fast. Hydra supports more than 30 protocols, including HTTP GET, HTTP HEAD, Oracle, pcAnywhere, rlogin, Telnet, SSH (v1 and v2 as well), and many, many more. As you might guess, THC Hydra is also implemented in zANTI2 and it eventually becomes an integral part of the app for its high functionality and usability. The zANTI2 developers named this section **Password Complexity Audit** and it is located under **Attack Actions** after a target is selected:

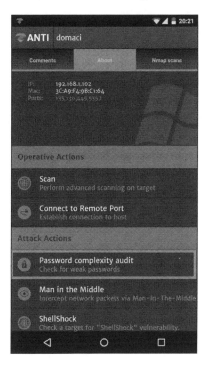

After selecting this option, you've probably noticed there are several types of attack. First, there are multiple dictionaries: **Small**, **Optimized**, **Big**, and a **Huge** dictionary that contains the highest amount of usernames and passwords.

To clarify, a dictionary attack is a method of breaking into a password-protected computer, service, or server by entering every word in a dictionary file as a username/password. Unlike a brute force attack, where any possible combinations are tried, a dictionary attack uses only those possibilities that are deemed most likely to succeed. Files used for dictionary attacks (also called wordlists) can be found anywhere on the Internet, starting from basic ones to huge ones containing more than 900,000,000 words for WPA2 WiFi cracking. zANTI2 also lets you use a custom wordlist for the attack:

Apart from dictionary attacks, there is an **Incremental** option, which is used for brute force attacks. This attempts to guess the right combination using a custom range of letters/numbers:

To set up the method properly, ensure the cracking options are correctly set. The area of searched combinations is defined by min-max charset, where min stands for minimum length of the password, max for maximum length, and charset for character set, which in our case will be defined as lowercase letters.

The **Automatic Mode**, as the description says, automatically matches the list of protocols with the open ports on the target.

To select a custom protocol manually, simply disable the **Automatic Mode** and select the protocol you want to perform the attack on:

In our case that would be the SSH protocol for cracking a password used to establish the connection on port 22.

Since incremental is a brute force method, this might take an extremely long time to find the right combination. For instance, the password *zANTI2-hacks* would take about 350 thousand years for a desktop PC to crack; there are 77 character combinations and 43 sextillion possible combinations. Therefore, it is generally better to use dictionary attacks for cracking passwords that might be longer than just a few characters. However, if you have a few thousand years to spare, feel free to use the brute force method.

If everything went fine, you should now be able to view the access password with the username. You can easily connect to the target by tapping the finished result using one of the installed SSH clients:

When connected, it's all yours. All Linux commands can be executed using the app and you now have the power to list directories, change the password, and more.

Although connecting to port 22 might sound spicy, there is more to be discovered.

Microsoft-DS port connection

The Microsoft-DS file-sharing port with number 445 is one of the biggest targets for hackers. This port is type **SMB (Server Message Block)**, meaning it operates as an application-layer network protocol and is mainly used for providing shared access to files, printers, and whatnot. This is one of the reasons this port is a favorite place for hackers—it allows the transfer of malicious content to remote machines:

Port **445** has been present in Windows systems since Windows 2000 and for most of the time stays open, which exposes the target to worms such as W32.Deloder or Iraqi worm, and of course, makes it vulnerable to the power of zANTI2.

After selecting the port you will be prompted (again) for a **Username** with a **Password**. These credentials are the same as the ones used to log in to your Windows station:

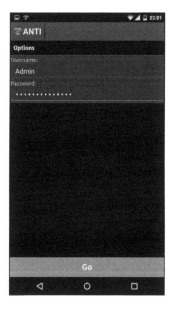

If these credentials are unknown to you, use the password-complexity audit once again to attempt to crack the password. Instead of applying the attack against the SSH protocol, choose the SMB protocol since this is an SMB port.

Tap **GO** to establish a connection:

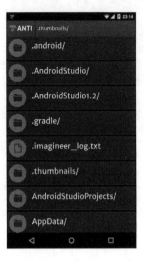

Since this port is used for file sharing and access, it is possible to display some parts of system and see the folders and files on it without the target even realizing.

This is very useful for viewing folders and files of a remote target through a local area network. Although it lets us investigate the target in an intrusive way, it still won't let us take full control over it. Let's look at Microsoft's Remote Desktop, the port number 3389.

A remote desktop connection

Microsoft has made a handy feature called **remote desktop**. As the title suggests, this lets an ordinary user access his home computer when he is away, or be used for managing a server through a network. This is a great sign that we can intercept this connection and exploit an open port to set up a remote desktop connection between our mobile phone and a target.

There is, however, one requirement. Since the **RDP (Remote Desktop Protocol)** port 3389 isn't open by default, a user has to allow connections from other computers. This option can be set in the control panel of Windows, and only then is port 3389 accessible.

If the option **Allow remote connections to this computer** is ticked on the victim's machine, we're good to go. This will leave the 3389 port open and listening for incoming broadcasts, including the ones from malicious attackers.

If we run a quick port discovery on the target, the remote desktop port with number 3389 will pop up. This is a good sign for us, indicating that this port is open and listening:

Tap the port (**ms-wbt-server**). You will be asked for login credentials once again. Tap **GO**.

Now, if you haven't got any remote desktop clients installed, zANTI2 will redirect you to Google Play to download one—the Parallels 2X RDP. This application, as you can tell, is capable of establishing remote desktop access from your Android device. It is stable, fast, and works very well.

After downloading the application, go back to zANTI2 and connect to the port once again. You will now be redirected directly to the app and a connection will be established immediately.

As you can see in the following screenshot, here's my computer—I'm currently working on the chapter! Apart from a simplified Windows user interface (using a basic XP look with no transparent bars and such), it is basically the same and you can take control over the whole system.

The Parallels 2X RDP client offers a comfortable and easy way to move the mouse and use the keyboard. However, while connecting to port 445 a victim has no idea about an intruder accessing the files on his computer; connecting to this port will log the current user out from the current session. However, if the remote desktop is set to allow multiple sessions at once, it is possible for a victim to see what the attacker currently controls.

The quality seems to be good, although the resolution is only 804 x 496 pixels 32-bit color depth. Despite these conditions, it is still easy to access folders, view files, or open applications.

As we can see in the practical demonstration, service ports should be accessible only by the authorized systems, not by anyone else. It is also a good way to teach you to secure login credentials on your machine to protect yourself not only from people behind your back but also mainly from people on the network.

Summary

In this chapter, we learned what open ports are and what dangers they expose to a machine that the port is open on. We also showed how a connection to these ports is established, how to crack password-protected ports, and how to access them afterwards using tools like ConnectBot or the remote desktop client.

In the next chapter, we will take a closer look at detecting and exploiting vulnerabilities in remote systems, servers, and services.

4
Vulnerabilities

Little holes in the system, when exploited, can ruin the whole network, exposing sensitive information, crashing and shutting down the machines. This is all because of one tiny insufficiency in a network, software, or a device—vulnerabilities.

In this chapter, you're going to:

- Learn what vulnerabilities are and how are they found
- Understand the basics of reverse engineering and their role in network security
- Learn how a vulnerability can be detected using zANTI2
- Learn how vulnerabilities are exploited using all possible tools

A vulnerability

Generally speaking, a vulnerability represents a certain kind of weakness, which, when exploited, allows an attacker to discover more about a system. This could mean reducing information assurance or exposing sensitive data. It is the same when it comes to computer security. Vulnerability is typically the intersection of three essential elements: a system susceptibility, an attacker with access to this susceptibility, and finally a skill required to be able to exploit this flaw.

Vulnerability can be described as:

> *"A weakness of an asset or group of assets that can be exploited by one or more threats."*

> - https://en.wikipedia.org/wiki/Vulnerability_%28computing%29

A vulnerability is thus defined as a weak link that provides at least one way of exploitation.

It is obvious that vulnerabilities are one of the biggest problems of today's network security worldwide. Without a doubt, they will be a huge problem in the future too. You may ask yourself, how is a vulnerability created, why can't there be systems and software with no vulnerabilities at all?

This is obviously what all the software manufacturers are trying to do—building the most resilient and vulnerability-free software for all. However, it is not that easy. There are plenty of ways to discover a remote vulnerability and often even easier ways to find a functional way to exploit it. Although it is definitely not an easy thing to do, tons of new vulnerabilities are found every year.

Reverse engineering

New, undiscovered vulnerabilities are often found using a process called reverse engineering. Although the title may be self-explanatory, let's have a closer look at what reverse engineering stands for.

Generally speaking, reverse engineering is the process of extracting information (basically from anything; it could be a building, software, or hardware) and reproducing it based on this information. Let's take an example of disassembling a LEGO building kit. What you do (probably without even realizing it) is that you use some kind of information about the subject and use this information to dig deeper, disassembling every LEGO part, leaving no parts connected. Then you use this information again to assemble the parts into something quite different, let's say an Android mascot.

Although this may sound weird reading all this in a penetration-testing book, it is absolutely the same for real penetration testing, finding and creating exploits for vulnerabilities.

Finding an exploitable vulnerability in a system or a piece of software isn't something that's easy or that you can do in a few minutes. Companies are not trying to build software that has no vulnerabilities in it but instead trying to find all the vulnerabilities before the malicious attackers do.

It is now common for big and high-level companies like Google to hire hackers to find remotely exploitable vulnerabilities in the system. For instance, Google has recently extended a vulnerability research program to Android, offering up to a $30,000 bounty for finding and successfully developing a patch for a vulnerability on Android OS.

> Hacker, commonly misplaced with cracker, describes people with high computer/network/programming skills. They are capable of detecting but also patching vulnerabilities in the system, fixing and improving the source code on websites and so on. These are called **white hats**. A white hat hacker does not invade software or systems for malicious or harmful purposes but instead to test the network's security and such. The opposite to white hat hackers are **black hat** hackers, or **crackers**. These are often computer specialists who violate computer security for personal gain, to hack into someone's bank account and transfer the money to himself, for instance. A few more terms used by the community are **grey hat**, **blue hat**, or **script kiddie**—which describes a person who breaks into a computer system by using automated tools written by others. For example, that teenager kid who's hacking people's Facebook accounts in school using tools like zANTI, could be referred to as a script kiddie.

Reverse engineering, however, isn't only meant to detect code errors and vulnerabilities but also to create them. I wouldn't call them vulnerabilities as these recompiled applications are directly meant to harm an end user, but apart from security, reverse engineering also plays a big role in creating malicious software.

For instance, the dex2jar, one of the most used Java decompiling software, has been turned into a real Android app, the **Show Java**. Show Java quickly decompiles (converts an executable ready to run an application into a form of programming language, in this case Java) any installed applications on your Android phone, showing the possible Java code translated from the `Classes.dex` file. Although Show Java doesn't let you change the source code of an app, only to view it, other tools do. This process, called **recompiling**, is used to firstly decompile, change the source code, and compile the whole software application afterwards, leaving only slight and often not visible changes to it, which are typically used to harm a user who uses this app.

The preceding screenshot shows the source code of a decompiled application.

Although this may sound unrelated to network penetration testing, it's basically the same thing. A similar process can also be used to detect vulnerabilities of a software application.

Code, code, and more code is usually what it takes to discover, patch, or exploit a hidden vulnerability in the system. Most companies nowadays use network vulnerability scanners that find already discovered vulnerabilities on the Internet. For example, one of the best-known vulnerability scanners is Nessus, which allows scans for remotely accessible vulnerabilities, misconfigurations, weak passwords, and more.

There are certainly many more undiscovered vulnerabilities to be found and eventually patched. For now, we're going to focus on those that are already out there and are ready to be exploited on remote machines, servers, and devices.

For most of the time, we will look at *Common Vulnerabilities and Exposures*, often marked as CVE. CVE offers a dictionary of publicly known information security vulnerabilities and exposures and is publicly available to view. The CVE reference numbers typically follow a number pattern indicating unique identifiers for each vulnerability (CVE-YYYY-NNNN, where YYYY indicates the year the ID is issued for this vulnerability and NNNN stands for the identifier). For instance, CVE-2012-1182, which is the code name for the Samba heap overflow vulnerability, allows remote code execution from an anonymous connection. This vulnerability can be detected using the code execution through the Nmap Scripting Engine inside zANTI2.

Vulnerabilities we're going to exploit using zANTI2 are often those that are found on obsolete and outdated software, browsers, and services. Exploiting old vulnerabilities in legacy software versions is without a doubt one of the easiest ways to hack into someone's PC. Not keeping an application's version up to date can be much more dangerous than you might think and might cause serious security issues, hacked accounts, viruses, and more, as you will see in the following examples.

Shellshock

Discovered in September 2014, Shellshock is a recent vulnerability in Unix Bash shell (Bash is a Unix shell and command language and is widely used by server deployments, computers, and such) that has spread across the globe at incredible speed. Security companies recorded millions of attacks in the days following the vulnerability disclosure. Shellshock was labeled as a very severe bug and was compared to the Heartbleed security bug that was disclosed in April 2014. If you've heard of Heartbleed, you probably know that this was a huge boom when it was discovered. Exploiting this vulnerability let anyone on the Internet encrypt the traffic, including names, passwords, and the actual content going through a connection.

The Shellshock bug is an example of an arbitrary code execution vulnerability. This term describes an attacker's ability to execute any commands on a target machine. It is the most powerful effect a bug can have because it lets an attacker take control over the target completely. You probably read about this in *Chapter 2, Scanning for Your Victim*, where some Nmap scripts let us detect this kind of vulnerability on a remote system.

This is how Shellshock *works*: if the characters " { : : , } ; are included as the function definition, basically any code that is inserted after this definition is processed. This isn't something that should happen and it lets an attacker execute any type of code because Bash will eventually execute this.

For instance, executing the code: `() {:;}; /bin/eject www.vulnerablesite.com`, would actually be enough to eject the CD/DVD drive. This gives you a quick idea of the severity of this bug. Since Shellshock is still a thing, it would be appropriate to scan your machine and detect whether you are vulnerable or not.

zANTI2 provides a way to quickly check if the target (local or remote) is vulnerable in just a few clicks. The scan option is visible under **Attack Actions**, because to find out the vulnerability an arbitrary code has to be executed on the target first. The scanning process works by sending a crafted HTTP request with a command-injecting payload. Then it simply checks the output.

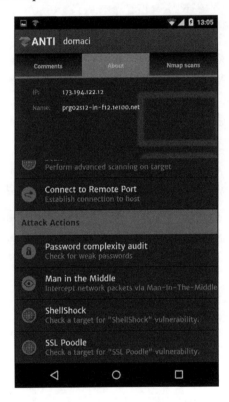

zANTI2 also allows for vulnerability checks outside of the local area network and lets you see if any web servers are vulnerable to any of the following vulnerabilities (Shellshock, SSL Poodle) as well.

To perform Shellshock detection on a remote machine out of the local area network, add any host IP from the action bar. The IP address of a website can easily be found by tracerouting or pinging it using a terminal emulator.

Fortunately, in most cases you'll find the target *not vulnerable* against the Shellshock vulnerability exploitation, thanks to a quick response from web server administrators and maintainers. However, if the target looks to be vulnerable, it might represent a huge danger for itself.

Zimperium has also built a Shellshock scanner for device and app vulnerability checks as an individual application, which can be downloaded for free on Google Play. This scanner determines whether your device is running Bash and if you have mobile applications that include the Bash process, which could be potentially dangerous by exposing your device to the Shellshock vulnerability. In other words, the Shellshock scanners try to connect to a port of the target, or wait for a reverse connection to a specific port, or create a sample file in an accessible path. However, even a vulnerable target that is well protected by a firewall may be vulnerable, because of the accessibility issues. These scanners are thus not 100 percent accurate and can also cause false negatives, but they're better than nothing.

Shellshock isn't the only bug zANTI2 is capable of detecting. You should've probably noticed that there is one more vulnerability called SSL Poodle.

SSL Poodle

Poodle, which literally stands for **Padding Oracle on Downgraded Legacy Encryption**, is a Man-In-The-Middle exploit that takes advantage of the way some browsers deal with encryption. Poodle can be used to target browser-based communication that relies on the Secure Sockets Layer 3.0 (SSL) protocol for authentication and encryption. SSL has in most cases been replaced by the **Transport Layer Security (TLS)** protocol, but some browsers will revert to SSL when a TLS connection isn't available.

When exploited, an attacker is capable of exposing encrypted information by standing between the sender and receiver (called MITM; more about this attack in the following chapter). The only way to prevent Poodle attacks is to stop using SSL 3.0. Use of this protocol among browsers is now minimal, though there might be cases where this protocol is still being used.

It took only one day for SSLv3-powered services to be moved to TLS, increasing from 3 percent to 11 percent worldwide from October 14 when the Poodle vulnerability was disclosed.

Zetasploit exploits

Let's take a look at some more vulnerabilities that can be exploited directly in zANTI2 using Zetasploit. Zetasploit offers a bunch of cloud exploits that can be remotely applied on your targets. Unfortunately, Zetasploit is only available to beta testers or to companies using the premium version that also allows you to create comprehensive security reports on devices on a network and many more features. Although you cannot directly exploit vulnerabilities through zANTI2 as a community user, it is possible to view whether a remote host is vulnerable or not, which gives you a quick idea of the target's security.

To see if there are any remotely exploitable vulnerabilities on the target, we need to intercept network packets first using an MITM attack. This attack is based on an intercepted connection between a victim (receiver) and a sender. The attacker literally stands between these two targets, masking himself by using spoofed public keys used by the sender and receiver, letting him see everything these two targets are sending between themselves. The MITM attack represents a great danger in open networks, and we will talk about this in the next chapter. For now, let's just use this option to detect remotely exploitable vulnerabilities on a remote system.

Choose a target you're going to check a vulnerability on and access the MITM window in **Attack Actions** of a host. I'll choose my computer as the target, which I'm going to use as a victim for the exploit.

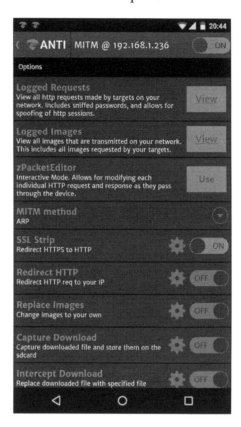

Enable the MITM attack on the top-right of the action bar. zANTI2 will now sniff through the network packets and start gathering collected information including pages the victim is browsing through, images he/she is viewing, and will also list service versions and other essential information that will help us see if there is any remote vulnerability.

Let's select the **Logged Requests** option to see all HTTP requests that went through us. This includes sessions, which can be forged and opened afterwards on our mobile devices, as well as the passwords or browser information, which is what we will be taking a look at now.

Let's skip other tabs. I'll cover these in the next chapter. Now, move right on to the **User Agents** tab. This provides us with information about the target browser, versions, and other OS details.

As you can see, there is an Internet Explorer exploit available. You can't do much more now as a community user of the application but for a full Zimperium user, things start to get much more interesting now. Zetasploit offers a ton of cloud exploits that can easily invade any vulnerable software using zANTI2 on your mobile device.

In this example, we are talking about the MS10-002 vulnerability, which is present on older browser versions, including Internet Explorer 8.

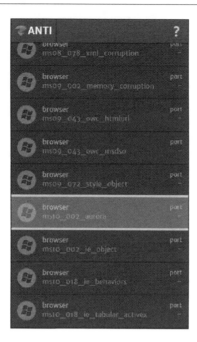

By exploiting this vulnerability, an attacker is capable of accessing the Windows system or Shell remotely by using the inbuilt VNC client in zANTI2, similarly as when connecting to Remote Desktop client port 3389.

When exploited, an attacker can either execute shell commands on the machine or simply control it using the VNC client, as shown in the following screenshot:

This lets any intruder quickly hack into a remote machine, all caused by using an old browser version.

Still ignoring those update requests from apps? Here's why you should always keep your software up to date. Since Zetasploit isn't something widely available for a daily user (at least not right now), it isn't possible to remotely exploit vulnerabilities and access systems using zANTI2. However, it is still a handy option to quickly see if the target you're attacking has any chance of exploits on the current browser version. Since Zetasploit uses Metasploit exploits (as you can tell by the name), the same thing can be done on your computer using this framework, but in terms of simplicity and comfort, nothing beats zANTI2.

Summary

In this chapter, we learned what a vulnerability is, where they can be found, how they are detected and finally exploited, more about Shellshock and Poodle vulnerabilities, and how you can quickly scan for these on local or remote machines using the zANTI2 app and how a browser vulnerability is exploited using cloud exploits provided by Zetasploit.

In the next chapter, we will take a look at Man-In-The-Middle attacks, which provide literally the easiest way to hack into someone's account, steal passwords, redirect victims to other websites, or inject scripts to a website by simply intercepting a network connection between two targets. Apart from this, we will learn more about how it is possible to protect yourself from these types of attacks by using an HTTPS-encrypted connection or using ARP spoofing detectors.

5
Attacking – MITM Style

We have reached the last chapter of this book, which undoubtedly is going to be the most interesting chapter. **Man-in-the-middle (MITM)** attacks are one of the biggest threats to any public network, they let anyone steal your personal data without your knowledge or freely control the traffic on the local area network. It's pretty simple.

In this chapter, you will learn the following:

- What is MITM, how it works, and how you can easily trigger this attack and intrude into anyone's computer on the **local area network (LAN)** using zANTI2.

- Things that you can do by taking advantage of this attack, including redirecting websites, injecting custom scripts on the websites, replacing images, and much more.

- More about protection against these types of attacks because after all, you could be the next victim! Also we'll have a look at the **Hyper Text Transfer Protocol Secure (HTTPS)** protocol, which is here to prevent these types of attacks but also shows how to bypass this security by performing an SSL Strip on a target.

Man in the middle?

So, as you probably read in previous chapters, you know that the MITM attack stands for **Man in the middle**. Although this might sound a bit out of key, it accurately expresses the substantiality of the whole thing. Let's see how this attack works.

Some of you might've heard about the Alice and Bob example, which explains what the MITM attack is based on. For those who are not familiar with this, let's say that there are two people—Alice and Bob. Alice tries to communicate with Bob by sending him a message. What they don't know is that there's an attacker trying to intercept and eavesdrop the whole conversation by performing the MITM attack on a network where these two people communicate on.

First, Alice asks Bob for his public key. Obviously, this doesn't happen in a normal conversation, but the public key is necessary in this case to establish a key-protected conversation between Alice and Bob. Public keys are typically used to encrypt plaintext (for example, text messages and documents) or to verify a digital signature. There is also a private key, which is used to decrypt the encrypted text or create a digital signature. In other words, the private key is used for the opposite operation as the public key is used for.

This key contains the algorithm for further encryption of any messages sent between Alice and Bob, so nobody except these two knows what messages they are sending. However, don't forget that there's an attacker on the network. The attacker is able to intercept this public key by launching an MITM attack and is now capable of not only viewing sent messages, but also modifying them by decrypting them using the key and encrypting them afterward.

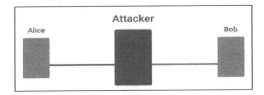

The preceding picture clearly shows how such an attack works. The attacker literally stands between two (or more) targets, intercepting network packets sent from Alice, modifying them and then sending the messages to Bob, who has no idea that the messages are being changed. Let's continue with our example:

Alice starts the conversation. She sends the following message:

Hey Bob, it's Alice – give me your key!

he conversation is already being intercepted by an attacker, which first arrives to him and then gets sent to Bob. He then responds:

Hi Alice, here's my key [Bob's key].

Since the attack cannot really intercept an encrypted conversation, he needs to know the key algorithm used for encrypting/decrypting messages. He does this by sending his own key instead of Bob's key to Alice, so he can easily decrypt and see the content of any further message sent between these two guys. The attacker slightly modifies the message as follows:

Hi Alice, here's my key [Attacker's key].

Alice encrypts the message thinking that it's the Bob's key and only he can read messages encrypted with this key. She sends a message:

How was your day? [encrypted with the attacker's key]

Alice thinks that she encrypted the message with Bob's key, so only he can decrypt and read it. However, in fact, the key was modified by the attacker, so he can decrypt and read it as well. The attacker will decrypt the message and re-encrypt it with Bob's key, so he doesn't spot anything.

How was your day? [encrypted with Bob's key]

The conversation goes on. Nobody spots a thing this way.

Attacks like this are generally possible against any message sent using public key technology. Public-key cryptography is based on algorithms that require two separate keys—private and public.

A large, random number is generated for keys that are suitable for use for the encryption. You can see on the picture, in an asymmetric key encryption scheme, anyone can encrypt messages using the public key, but only the holder of the private key can decrypt them. Therefore, security of the entire communication depends on the secrecy of the private key.

In this case, the attacker takes advantage of intercepted private key security and easily reads or modifies messages from Alice or Bob based on each other's keys as follows. It's that easy:

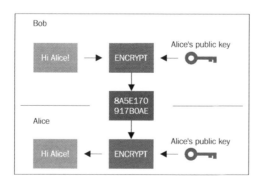

Various defenses against MITM attacks use additional authentication techniques that include **Domain Name System Security Extensions (DNSSEC)**, public key infrastructures (using digital certificates and public-key encryption), certificate pinning (which detects and blocks many kinds of MITM attacks and adds an extra step beyond the normal X.509 certificate validation), stronger mutual authentication, secret better-encrypted keys, and many more. One of the defenses you can come across using MITM on a network is a router firewall, which can block various types of connections, preventing you from a successful MITM attack.

ARP spoofing

ARP spoofing (or ARP poisoning) is one of the most used methods to spy on the web traffic and intercept network packages in real time. This is also the method we will use for our MITM attacks with zANTI2.

Address Resolution Protocol (ARP) is a protocol used in LAN to resolve MAC addresses of the next or final destination IP. It's a method of letting the network map out IPs rather than giving each computer a table of the mapping. This protocol is vulnerable to poisoning because there is no method of checking the authenticity of ARP replies, so they can be spoofed from other addresses on the network. An attacker sends a spoofed ARP messages onto a LAN, trying to associate his MAC / IP address, which will cause the traffic meant for that IP to be sent to him instead of the original recipient. ARP spoofing allows an attacker to intercept data frames on a network, modify the traffic or, as I'll show later, to stop the traffic completely. This kind of an attack will (in our case) be used as an opening for the MITM attack on a local network, attacking, and poisoning our victim to modify the traffic as shown in the following image:

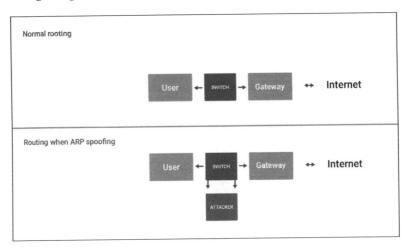

A successful ARP spoofing attack allows an attacker to alter routing on a network, which allows for an MITM attack. This is what we will use ARP spoofing for.

Although we will use the ARP method for our further attacks, there is one more available in zANTI2, in the MITM options of the app as shown in the following image:

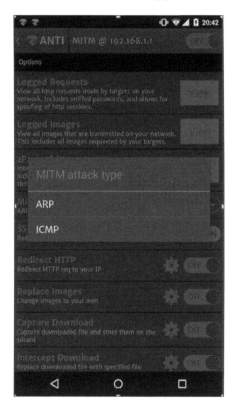

ICMP stands for **Internet Control Message Protocol** and is one of the most used protocols in networking technology. It is typically used by network devices, such as routers, to send error messages (that a service is not available or a host can't be reached for example).

An ICMP MITM attack is accomplished by spoofing an ICMP redirect message to any router between the victim and the server. The biggest advantage of ICMP attacks is that it does not require LAN access, but on the other hand, many routers do not accept ICMP redirect packets.

Zimperium security research, however, has disclosed a new type of MITM attack that is being widely exploited by hackers all around the world. It's a type of ICMP redirect attack and is named **DoubleDirect**. This attack enables an attacker to redirect a victim's traffic to the attacker's device, steal personal information, and deliver malicious payloads to the victim's device pretty easily. DoubleDirect uses ICMP redirect packets to modify routing tables of a host. This method is legitimately used by routers to notify the hosts that a better route is available for a particular destination. However, when exploited, an attacker can use the packets to alter the tables on the victim, resulting in launching an MITM attack.

This being said, zANTI2 does support full-duplex MITM using the ICMP redirect, but we'll use the ARP poisoning method for its usability, flexibility, and the presence of more victims vulnerable to this method (since many devices do not support ICMP redirects).

MITM attacks through zANTI2

zANTI2 brings MITM to the next level. It takes advantage of intercepted network packets sent through the network and lets an attacker modify, read, or forge requests individually, inject script code to a website, or just cut the connection globally on the whole network. Let's have a look at how these functions work, how they are triggered, and their use.

First, let's see how to start the attack on one of your victims:

The example showing the basics of MITM launched between Alice and Bob gives us an idea of how a secure connection is intercepted between two subjects. However, this is not enough for us. We want to sniff through the entire network, no matter how many connections there are and how many people are browsing the Net, typing passwords, or communicating. We want to intrude into all of them.

To do so, instead of selecting an individual device, we will tap on the main router (192.168.1.1) or select the entire network field with 192.168.1.1/24. This is known as **Classless Inter-Domain Routing (CIDR)**, which is a method for allocating and routing IP packets. If selected, all 192.168.1.* will be scanned and affected while attacking. After selecting the victim, we can see the following screen:

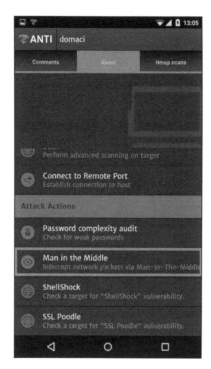

Select the **Man In The Middle** option under **Attack Actions** of your selected host/router/subnet mask. This will open up the following window activity:

Let's have a look at each option zANTI2 has to offer. Although listening to someone's connection might sound cool, there's much more to do. We're going to start with the basics.

Logged requests

As the description says, this option lets you view all HTTP requests made by targets on the network. You may wonder at why only HTTP requests can be viewed. This is because HTTPS is based on advanced cryptography including certificate checks that stops us from logging and hijacking sessions of a victim. I'll explain how we will bypass this protocol by using the SSL Strip HTTPS redirection on the following pages:

In short, logged requests will list the following things:

- Requested URLs by the target
- Date, time, and number of requests made to the URL

- Passwords and usernames in plaintext (non-encrypted)

- Session cookies details

- Browser version and available exploits to vulnerabilities (using Zetasploit, as shown in the previous chapter)

Logged requests also lets you forge sessions based on requests made to the URLs and cookies. These requests can also be modified individually using ZPacketEditor before sending them to the host. But first things first. Let's have a look at how individual requests are shown inside of zANTI2 before modifying them:

As you can see on the picture, zANTI2 provides a list of all requested URLs (the sites your victim browses through), making it easy to filter each site by viewing the thumbnail that represents the website. There also is an exact URL address that's been requested by a network user and local IP address related to each request.

You've probably noted that the **passwords** field is right below of each request. Since HTTP protocol isn't well secured and passwords are not encrypted (thus sent as a simple plaintext), it is possible to easily extract all passwords typed into the passwords field on any website as shown in the following screenshot:

If there are any passwords found, zANTI2 prints them all for you and colors the request yellow for easy distinction. More options show up when this request is selected:

The first tab, **Sessions**, prints all the logged sessions of a particular HTTP request, along with the number of stored passwords and requests for each session and browser user agents. This information may be useful for further victim investigation, for example, an attacker can estimate and find possible exploits for the victim by looking at browser version, operating system, the device itself or build version.

Clicking one of the sessions will directly forge it inside zANTI2 and hijack the session with all its information, as follows:

Forged sessions basically take all the information provided by a victim (including cookies, passwords, and other data) to successfully create a web request from your device. You can see a Facebook page forged from a victim on my device—simple and fast. What's also great is that all the information, including intercepted packets, cookies, passwords, and other necessary data needed to forge a request are stored and can be accessed anytime, even outside the LAN. It lets you access old sessions from your victims any time you want.

Let's move on to the next tab, which is the **Passwords** tab. As the title suggests, this tab will show login credentials, including the username and password itself for any website. As said, the HTTP protocol does not encrypt passwords and sends them as simple text, which is what zANTI2 takes advantage of:

As you can see, the login credentials are saved and displayed in the form **Username:password** (example@example.com:1234). There is also the exact request made from the victim, which in this case points to a Facebook login page verification. Note the **POST** text right next to the URL address—a **POST** is a type of HTTP request and is used to send data to the server, such as customer information and file upload.

All of the information, including passwords are saved in zANTI2 and can be accessed anytime.

Let's have a look at the **Requests** tab, which shows every single HTTP request made by the victim. HTTP requests are sent by an HTTP client to a server in the form of a request message that typically includes a request line, an HTTP header, and optionally a message body. In zANTI2, it's a request message including the request address, request parameters, and headers:

If you have a closer look, you can see that each request has its own request type. Request types or methods indicate the method to be performed on the resource. We distinguish eight different methods:

- **GET**: This method is used to retrieve information from a server. These requests only retrieve data and don't send any.

- **HEAD**: This method is the same as GET, but it only transfers the status line and the header section. In other words, the server must not return a message body in the response.

- **POST**: A POST request, as mentioned, is used to send data to the server, including information, username, and other stuff using HTML forms.

- **PUT**: These requests replace all the current representations of the target resource with the newly uploaded content.

- **DELETE**: A DELETE request removes all the current representations of the target resource.

- **CONNECT**: This establishes a tunnel to the server.

- **OPTIONS**: This represents a request for information about the communication options.

- **TRACE**: This method is used to invoke a remote loop of the request message. This allows the client to see what is being received and use this data for diagnostic and testing information.

Let's have a look at **REQUEST HEADER** fields, shown in the preceding image. These allow the client to send additional information about the request and the client itself (for example, user agent and OS version) to the server. The most commonly used fields are:

- **ACCEPT**: The **ACCEPT** field can be used to specify certain media types that are acceptable for the response. For instance, `ACCEPT: AUDIO/*; q=0,2, AUDIO/BASIC` can be translated into `I prefer audio/basic but send me any audio type if it is the best available after an 80% markdown in quality`.

- **COOKIES**: This shows us further information about the HTTP cookie request. Note that there are two header fields — DPR and RW. The **DPR** header field that indicates the client's current **Device Pixel Ratio**. This is the ratio between physical and logical pixels. For example, iPhone 4 and 4S reports a DPR of 2 because the physical linear resolution (960 x 640) is double the logical resolution (480 x 320). The **RW** field is a number that indicates the **Resource Width**.

- **HOST**: This field specifies the Internet host. In our case, it's Facebook.

- **ACCEPT-LANGUAGE**: This field is a type and very similar to Accept header (which specifies media types). The **ACCEPT-LANGUAGE** header, as you can tell, restricts the set of languages that are preferred as a response to the request. In our case, the request header specifies **EN-US** language as the one that should be used.

- **X-REQUESTED-WITH**: This is mainly used to identify Ajax requests. Ajax is a group of web development techniques used to create asynchronous web applications. As you can see in the image, the field contains **COM.ANDROID. BROWSER** package, which Android system typically sends as information to the website to determine whether the client uses Android's browser application or a WebView activity.

- **CONTENT-TYPE**: This indicates the MIME type of the body. MIME or Internet media type is an identifier used to indicate the type OD data that a file contains.

- **ORIGIN**: Origin asks the server for an Access-Control-Allow-Origin response field, thus initiates a request for cross-origin resource sharing (CORS). CORS allows restricted resources, such as JavaScript, or fonts to be requested from another domain outside the domain from which the resource originated.

- **CONTENT-LENGTH**: This shows the length of the request body in 8-bit bytes (octets).

- **REFERER**: This field specifies the address of the previous web page from which a link to the currently requested page was followed. (And yes, it's **REFERER**, thanks to the spell error in the publication of the Internet Engineering Task Force's **RFC (Request for Comments)** publication).

- **USER-AGENT**: This shows the user agent string. When a software agent operates in a network, it commonly identifies its application type, software vendor, and operating system. This particular request is typically used for statistical purposes or automated recognition of user agents to avoid any limitations.

- **CONNECTION**: This field controls and specifies options for the currently established connection and list of request fields. **KEEP-ALIVE** request or HTTP persistent connection uses a single TCP connection to send or receive multiple requests/responses, as opposed to opening a new connection for every single request/response pair.

zANTI2 gives you the option to take all this information and forge this request with all of its headers and information to create a session that opens as a browser window. This lets you hijack a session quickly and easily without gathering any further information from the victim:

The **User Agent** tab, as shown in the previous chapter, takes advantage of available browser vulnerabilities and exploits them using Zetasploit.

Let's move on to the next feature, which is the **Logged Picture** section as shown in the following screenshot. As you can see, this simply takes all of the logged images from your victim and shows them to you (they also get saved into your gallery with a new album called z_images.

ZPacketEditor

Another pretty interesting and useful feature is called ZPacketEditor. As the description says, this allows us to modify each individual HTTP request and response as they pass through the device.

ZPacketEditor takes advantage of an ongoing MITM attack and stops sending any requests to the Internet unless you *confirm* them. The victim will not be able to access any websites unless you give him the permission to do so. We have the following image:

Every single request is displayed and gets ready for your interaction when the ZPacketEditor is turned on. You have two options now. Either you swipe your finger to the left, which will *approve* the incoming request and continue to send it to the web or you can swipe your finger to the right, which will let you individually edit the current request.

When a website loads, there are many types of requests made to the web when the page is finally loaded. For instance, there are numerous scripts, ads, website thumbnails, and more as shown in the preceding image. With ZPacketEditor turned on, you have the power to not only see all of these requests but also edit their values, headers, data, and type of the request. If you don't want the victim to send or receive the request at all, just don't. ZPacketEditor offers a brand new way to control anyone's connection easily and interactively.

Let's take an example of how to easily redirect an incoming request to another website by changing the host header field:

Each time your victim wants to visit a website, a **GET** request is sent to load the necessary information and data. This request contains common headers, such as user-agent, connection, language, and the `host` attribute.

Let's change the host field from `www.youtube.com` to `www.facebook.com` and hit **Send** to confirm the request. Instead of loading YouTube, the victim's machine will appear to have requested Facebook and load this page instead:

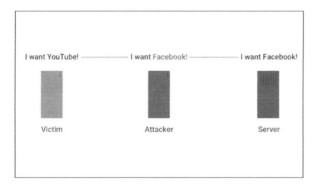

However, ensure the modified requests are sent in time. The victim's machine will most likely print a **time-out** error if the connection isn't reached for a specified amount of time.

Modifying individual network packets is a nice way to showcase the basic function of an MITM attack. Let's proceed to the next packet.

SSL Strip

You might've noticed that one of the functions was enabled the whole time by default. It's SSL Strip, and it is also one of the most important (if not the most important) things and if it wasn't there and enabled, none of the MITM features would work.

To point out the meaning of SSL Strip clearly, let's start with HTTP and HTTPS protocols. You've probably noted something like this on your browser's URL bar:

This indicates the connection to the website you're visiting is private and HTTPS secured. Is that a big deal? Actually, yes it is. The HTTPS effectively keeps your data secure using an encrypted connection on a **Secure Sockets Layer** (**SSL**) to send the information back and forth. Even if anyone between the sender and the recipient could open the message that's being sent, they still could not understand it because it is encrypted with a special code that only the original subjects of the communication can understand. No certificates are required for validation in case of HTTP, but on the other hand, HTTPS requires a special SSL digital certificate—apart from the data encryption.

This makes it pretty difficult for packet sniffing. In other words, we don't want our victim to browse through HTTPS-secured protocol. This would make it impossible for us to intercept, control, and modify the network packets. So, what do we do now? It's simple. We're going to strip the HTTPS protocol into HTTP:

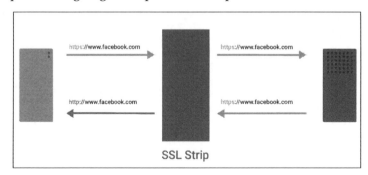

SSL Strip

As you can see on the picture, the SSL Strip changes the HTTPS protocol into simple HTTP protocol from a web server response. Having said this, the SSL Strip is a type of MITM attack although it's pretty innocent at first.

When a victim sends login credentials (to log in to Facebook for instance), they are all encrypted with HTTPS. However, the HTTP protocol does not encrypt any data, thus all information or password included are sent as plaintext. This makes it extremely easy to retrieve it from packets and requests.

If you take a look at the description of the SSL Strip as shown in the following image, it says **Visiting an https site directly will be unaffected**. This is pretty important because an SLL Strip cannot affect a direct HTTPS request:

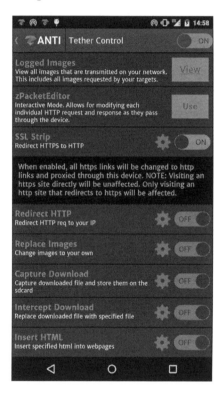

If you type `https://www.facebook.com` directly into your browser, a secured HTTPS connection will be established, no matter if an attacker runs SSL Strip on the network. However, clicking the Facebook link from an HTTP website will not make it HTTPS. So always have a look at the URL bar before hitting the login button.

HTTP redirection

This feature does basically the same thing as we showed with ZPacketEditor, but it does it faster and is easier to control. Input the website URL you want the victim to be redirected to and enable the function. Again, this only works on HTTP requests, and HTTPS URLs stay safe.

Replacing images

A spicy feature for changing every single picture into the one you choose is image replacement. This is pretty simple. Choose the image you want, and enable the function.

A Google search for dogs would then look like this:

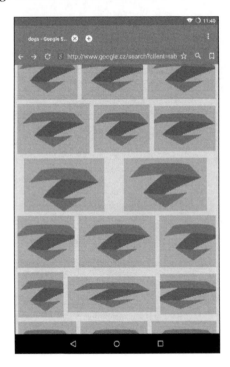

Capture/intercept downloads

Another little MITM feature that lets you capture a specific type of file your victim is downloading and optionally intercept it with your (possibly malicious) file for further interaction with the victim.

File types are: .apk (Android installation package), .exe (executable file for Windows, DOS, and so on), .doc (word file format), .xls (excel format), .pdf (portable document format), .mp3 (audio format), and .zip (archive file format). They are shown as follows:

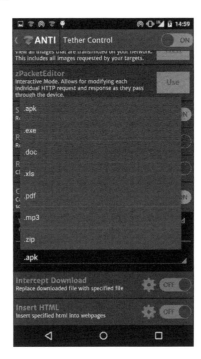

Insert HTML

The last MITM feature zANTI2 has to offer is **Insert HTML**, which inserts a specified code into web pages. By default, there's a simple script code triggering an alert window as follows:

```
<script>alert("Your text")</script>
```

After a successful injection, every web page will seem to pop an alert window when refreshed or loaded. Following is an injected JavaScript in the form of an alert window displays to user:

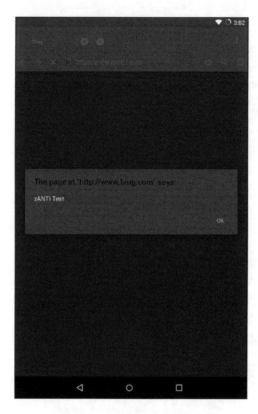

JavaScripts can be injected too and let you literally play with your victim. For instance, the following code rotates every single image on the current web page:

```
<script type="text/javascript">

window.onload=function() {
    rotate();
}

function rotate() {
    \$("img").rotate(180);
    \$(":image").rotate(180);
}
</script>
```

JavaScripts can be fun—decrease/increase text size, add a song playing in the background of every page, make the text on pages dance, all this and maybe more is possible with this cool feature.

It seems to be the last thing zANTI2 has to offer to us, but there are obviously many more ways to take advantage of intercepting network packages. For example, dSploit, the zANTI predecessor has brought a brand new way to control a victim's communication by replacing text on web pages:

Changing a single word *Android* to *Potato* could then lead to a great confusion on the other side. This is an ultimate way to troll and show that computer security is still a big problem when it comes to the unencrypted connection. It's not necessary to refer to open/public networks and the security of them. Next time you sign in to Starbucks WiFi, have this chapter in your mind because anybody can be the attacker. Stay secure!

Summary

In this chapter, we learned what an MITM is and how it works. We also showed how to launch and hijack sessions using zANTI2 using this attack, modify packets, redirect websites, replace images, or intercept files on a victim's computer to control targets on a network. We learned more about security, difference between protocols, why it's so important to use a secure connection and possible ways of protection against MITM attacks.

It looks like our journey has come to an end. I really do hope that your knowledge about penetration tests, zANTI2, vulnerabilities, or attacks has increased after reading this book and you found all the chapters useful, educational, and possibly entertaining. I want to thank you for purchasing this book and having interest in it. It's been a joyful ride, for me at least. Thank you.

Index

D

device type 35
DHCP (Dynamic Host Configuration
    Protocol) 49
Domain Name System (DNS) 40
Domain Name System Security
    Extensions (DNSSEC) 88
DPR (Device Pixel Ratio) 99
Dropbox
  URL 49
dSploit
  features 20

F

Facebook
  URL 105
fields, zANTI2
  defining 98, 99
File Transfer Protocol (FTP) 25, 46, 51

G

Geobytes
  URL 46
Geoplugin
  URL 46
grey hat 75

H

host scripts 43
Hyper Text Transfer Protocol Secure
    (HTTPS) protocol 85

I

ICMP (Internet Control Message
    Protocol) 89
info scripts
  Bitcoinrpc-info 50
  Broadcast-upnp-info 51
  Cassandra-info 50
  Cups-info 51
  Ipv6-node-info 50

  Metaploit-info 51
  Mysql-info 51
  Quake3-info 51
intense scan
  about 30-33
  OS detection 33-35
  types 33
Internet Protocol (IP) 32
intrusive scripts
  Distcc-cve2004-2687 52
  Domino-enum-users 51
  Firewall-bypass 51
  Jdwp-inject 51
  Samba-vuln-cve-2012-1182 51
IP/ICMP scan 40, 41
IP ID sequence generation 37, 38
IPv6 (Internet Protocol Version 6) 50

L

LDAP (Lightweight Directory Access
    Protocol) 46
local area network (LAN) 25
logged requests
  defining 92

M

man-in-the-middle (MITM)
  about 85
  ARP spoofing 88-90
  defining 85-87
methods, logged requests
  CONNECT 97
  DELETE 97
  GET 97
  HEAD 97
  OPTIONS 98
  POST 97
  PUT 97
  TRACE 98
Microsoft-DS port connection
  defining 66-68
MITM attacks, through zANTI2
  capture/intercept downloads 107

Thank you for buying
Learning zANTI2 for Android Pentesting

About Packt Publishing

Packt, pronounced 'packed', published its first book, *Mastering phpMyAdmin for Effective MySQL Management*, in April 2004, and subsequently continued to specialize in publishing highly focused books on specific technologies and solutions.

Our books and publications share the experiences of your fellow IT professionals in adapting and customizing today's systems, applications, and frameworks. Our solution-based books give you the knowledge and power to customize the software and technologies you're using to get the job done. Packt books are more specific and less general than the IT books you have seen in the past. Our unique business model allows us to bring you more focused information, giving you more of what you need to know, and less of what you don't.

Packt is a modern yet unique publishing company that focuses on producing quality, cutting-edge books for communities of developers, administrators, and newbies alike. For more information, please visit our website at www.packtpub.com.

About Packt Open Source

In 2010, Packt launched two new brands, Packt Open Source and Packt Enterprise, in order to continue its focus on specialization. This book is part of the Packt Open Source brand, home to books published on software built around open source licenses, and offering information to anybody from advanced developers to budding web designers. The Open Source brand also runs Packt's Open Source Royalty Scheme, by which Packt gives a royalty to each open source project about whose software a book is sold.

Writing for Packt

We welcome all inquiries from people who are interested in authoring. Book proposals should be sent to author@packtpub.com. If your book idea is still at an early stage and you would like to discuss it first before writing a formal book proposal, then please contact us; one of our commissioning editors will get in touch with you.

We're not just looking for published authors; if you have strong technical skills but no writing experience, our experienced editors can help you develop a writing career, or simply get some additional reward for your expertise.

Python Web Penetration Testing Cookbook

ISBN: 978-1-78439-293-2   Paperback: 224 pages

Over 60 indispensable Python recipes to ensure you always have the right code on hand for web application testing

1. Get useful guidance on writing Python scripts and using libraries to put websites and web apps through their paces.

2. Find the script you need to deal with any stage of the web testing process.

3. Develop your Python knowledge to get ahead of the game for web testing and expand your skillset to other testing areas.

Kali Linux Wireless Penetration Testing: Beginner's Guide

ISBN: 978-1-78328-041-4   Paperback: 214 pages

Master wireless testing techniques to survey and attack wireless networks with Kali Linux

1. Learn wireless penetration testing with Kali Linux; Backtrack's evolution.

2. Detect hidden wireless networks and discover their names.

3. Explore advanced Wi-Fi hacking techniques including rogue access point hosting and probe sniffing.

4. Develop your encryption cracking skills and gain an insight into the methods used by attackers and the underlying technologies that facilitate these attacks.

Please check **www.PacktPub.com** for information on our titles

Mastering Wireless Penetration Testing for Highly Secured Environments

ISBN: 978-1-78216-318-3   Paperback: 220 pages

Scan, exploit, and crack wireless networks by using the most advanced techniques from security professionals

1. Conduct a full wireless penetration test and implement defensive techniques that can be used to protect wireless systems.

2. Crack WEP, WPA, and even WPA2 wireless networks.

3. A hands-on guide teaching how to expose wireless security threats through the eyes of an attacker.

Python Penetration Testing Essentials

ISBN: 978-1-78439-858-3   Paperback: 178 pages

Employ the power of Python to get the best out of pentesting

1. Learn to detect and avoid various types of attacks that put the privacy of a system at risk.

2. Employ practical approaches to penetration testing using Python to build efficient code and eventually save time.

3. Enhance your concepts about wireless applications and information gathering of a web server.

Please check **www.PacktPub.com** for information on our titles

Made in the USA
San Bernardino, CA
27 December 2015